Vico and Literary Mannerism

Emory Vico Studies

Donald Phillip Verene
General Editor

Vol. 6

PETER LANG
New York • Washington, D.C./Baltimore • Boston
Bern • Frankfurt am Main • Berlin • Vienna • Paris

Leo Catana

Vico and Literary Mannerism

A Study in the Early Vico and His Idea of Rhetoric and Ingenuity

PETER LANG
New York • Washington, D.C./Baltimore • Boston
Bern • Frankfurt am Main • Berlin • Vienna • Paris

Library of Congress Cataloging-in-Publication Data

Catana, Leo.
[Vico og barokkens retorik.]
Vico and literary mannerism: a study in the early Vico and
his idea of rhetoric and ingenuity / Leo Catana.
p. cm. — (Emory Vico studies; vol. 6)
Includes bibliographical references (p.   ) and index.
1. Vico, Giambattista, 1668–1744—Contributions in philosophy of rhetoric.
2. Rhetoric—Philosophy—History—17th century. I. Title. II. Series.
P85.V53C3813   808'.001—DC21   97-40824
ISBN 0-8204-3963-0
ISSN 0883-6000

Die Deutsche Bibliothek-CIP-Einheitsaufnahme

Catana, Leo:
Vico and literary mannerism: a study in the early Vico and his idea of rhetoric
and ingenuity / Leo Catana. –New York; Washington, D.C./Baltimore;
Boston; Bern; Frankfurt am Main; Berlin; Vienna; Paris: Lang.
(Emory Vico studies; Vol. 6)
ISBN 0-8204-3963-0

The paper in this book meets the guidelines for permanence and durability
of the Committee on Production Guidelines for Book Longevity
of the Council of Library Resources.

Printed in the United States of America

To Andrea Battistini

Acknowledgements

This work is a translated version of parts of a Danish book, *Vico og barokkens retorik*, published in Copenhagen in 1996 by Museum Tusculanum in the series *Studier for Sprog– og Oldtidsforskning*. I should like to thank the editor of this series, Minna Skafte Jensen, for permission to publish parts of that book in English. Likewise, I wish to acknowledge the support of the trust Dr. phil. Leif Nedergaard, which has made an English publication possible.

In the early days, I had several conversations with Andrea Battistini and Carl Henrik Koch about Vico, and I should like to thank both of them in this connection. I have also discussed the present English version with Kristian Jensen and Jill Kraye, whom I should like to thank for their advice. The appendix of this work provides new translations of the texts of two Italian mannerists, and I owe many thanks to Laura Orsi for her careful assistance in relation to these translations. I also wish to thank Lucy McGuinness, Will Stenhouse, Sophie Page, Jonathan Rolls and Celine Haastrup for their kind help.

Contents

Preface

Can thought and language be regarded as separable? Plato understood the philosopher as someone who desires to know reality in its highest forms, but also as one whose thought is unable fully to reach this reality, and who therefore longs for it even more strongly. At the same time Plato had warned this philosopher against the allurement of poets' elegant language, since it marks nothing but insight into the art of imitating with metre, rhythm and music; not into this higher reality, or truth, itself (*Symposium* 200–204; *Republic* 601). Words were conceived by Plato as a clothing of thought, sometimes a fraudulent clothing, wherefore stylistic sensibility and creativity became secondary to the philosopher.

This separation between thought and language, established by Plato, is traceable throughout the history of philosophy. The Italian philosopher Giambattista Vico (1668–1744) was living in an epoch in which the mode of expression was cultivated, but not, as Plato said, in order to neglect reality: language was regarded as inseparable from thoughts about reality, and language, as tangible signs, was consequently conceived as a means to grasp reality. This was the central idea among the theoreticians of the literary mannerism in Italy, Matteo Peregrini (1595–1652) and Emanuele Tesauro (1592–1675).

Vico was inspired by these theoreticians, and when the influential French rationalist René Descartes (1596–1650) and his followers affirmed the doctrine of Plato, Vico tried to elaborate and defend the idea of mannerism against the persisting Cartesians. The concept of *ingenium*, ingenuity, takes up a decisive role in Vico's counterattack, because it signifies a faculty of cognition acting through this condemned, linguistic sensibility. The idea of ingenuity advanced by Vico is also central in the tradition of rhetoric, in which language and thought are regarded as intimately bound to each other, and Vico was strongly indebted to it.

Introduction

Vico's defence of the tradition of rhetoric was not a defence of a mere academic discipline—it was a self–defence as well, since the story of his life was inextricably linked with the idea of rhetoric particular to his time. He was born in Naples in 1668 as the sixth child in a family with eight children. His father owed a small book shop. When Vico was seven years old, he fell off a staircase and had to postpone his school attendance for three years, until the convalescence was over. He was taught at school from the age of ten to eighteen, but these years were characterised by interruptions and changing schools and teachers. At the age of sixteen he began studying civil and canonical law at the university of Naples, but this study too was far from continuous and steady: Vico turned out to be a clever, impatient and wilful student, who, according to his autobiography, often left the class room in order to study on his own. Two years after he had started studying law, he had to interrupt it, because he wanted to take up a job as private teacher at Vatolla, a castle outside Naples. He managed, however, to finish his studies in the meanwhile, and at the age of twenty–six he graduated in civil and canonical law. The following year he left the job as a private teacher. These years spent at Vatolla, from his eighteenth to his twenty–seventh year, were important, since during these years he gained a vast and personal relationship to Italian philosophy and literature.

Apart from attending lessons in law, Vico frequently went to Naples in order to take part in the social and intellectual life there. At that time, Naples was a melting pot for philosophical and scientific theories, and Vico was in contact with many important intellectuals of the time. Among these were some of those who had a positive attitude towards the new experimental science, and who were subsequently convicted of atheism by the Inquisition. Vico also took part, even actively, in many of the recitations for nobles and ecclesiasticals. Shortly after Vico gave up his job at Vatolla, he returned to Naples, where he married, had a family and started teaching rhetoric at the faculty of law. In 1723, when Vico was fifty–five years old, he applied for a job as teacher in jurisprudence, a job which was more esteemed and better paid, but he was rejected for the position and remained a teacher of rhetoric until a few years before his death in 1744.[1]

So, Vico had encountered two different versions of rhetoric: Through recitations he had experienced, and practised, a kind of rhetoric which was widely diffused at the time, namely rhetoric as an art of writing occasional poems and eulogies; and through his teaching in rhetoric at the faculty of law, he knew rhetoric as a theory of argumentation, used in juridical processes. In this book I shall attempt to explain Vico's position regarding these two versions of rhetoric. Until recently, Vico's interest in rhetoric has often been discarded among scholars as insignificant to his philosophy—instead, they have traditionally paid attention to Vico's philosophy of history, his *Scienza nuova* (New Science), dating from 1725.[2] But I think that these formative years of Vico, in which he assimilated the tradition of rhetoric, may be of interest for anyone seeking to understand his philosophy, even in relation to the *Scienza nuova*, since certain rhetorical concepts continue to play an important role throughout his authorship.

As a teacher in rhetoric at the university in Naples, from 1699 till 1741, it was the duty of Vico to write a manual for his lectures.[3] Vico did not find this manual worthy of mentioning in his autobiography, *Vita*, dating from 1725, or in the lists of his works which were attached to the two subsequent editions of *Vita*, in 1728 and in 1734.[4] Nevertheless, this manual contains the most important reflections on the literary mannerism and its aesthetic theory. This track has been blurred, even more than it was already, by the poor edition by Giovanni Gentile and Fausto Nicolilni of this manual, severely abbreviated and translated from Latin into Italian. Despite the fact that Vico's manual in rhetoric chronologically belongs to the first part of his authorship, it was placed in the last volume in this complete edition. The editorial decisions can be explained by the idealistic interpretation of Vico's authorship, on which Nicolini based the first complete edition of Vico's works, published from 1914 to 1941, according to which Vico's occupation with rhetoric was not regarded as philosophically important. In 1941 Nicolini noted in the comments to this last volume, that the manual did not have any philosophical significance—at best only a biographical one. Consequently, he asked whether these pages from the manual,

> ...contain anything but passages from Cicero, Cesare, Sallust and other Latin writers, quoted more or less at length, to which examples are added. And, again, many other pages wasted on nothing but popular definitions and divisions, repeated innumerable times and often with the same formulations by Vico—definitions and divisions from numberless schoolbooks, published and in the form of manuscripts, from the seventeenth and the eighteenth century?[5]

Presumably Vico had worked out such a manual for the first time in 1699, but the earliest version we know of today dates from 1711, and stems from two identical copies, probably written down by students, on the following pages called *Institutiones oratoriae* (Textbook in Rhetoric).[6]

This manual contains the paragraph *De sententiis, vulgo 'del ben parlare in concetti'* (On Sayings, Popularly Called 'to Speak in Aphorisms'),[7] in which you find definitions of ingenuity, acuteness and a theory on metaphor. Vico explicitly mentions Aristotle's *Rhetoric* and *Poetics* as sources of these definitions, but there is no reason to believe that Vico himself had found them in the writings of Aristotle, since the same definitions and examples were widely used by other and earlier theoreticians in the movement of literary mannerism in Italy: By Matteo

Peregrini in his *Delle acutezze, che altrimenti spiriti, vivezze e concetti volgarmente si appellano* (On *Acutezze*, which are Commonly Called Lively Wits, Vivacities and Conceits), published in 1639; by Sforza Pallavicino, who in 1646 published *Trattato dello stile e del dialogo* (Treatise on Style and on Dialogue); and by Emanuele Tesauro in his *Il cannocchiale aristotelico* (The Aristotelian Telescope), which was well–known and published many times, the first one dating from 1654.

Considering that the ideas about ingenuity and metaphor, well described in *Institutiones oratoriae*, remain central in the rest of Vico's authorship, it seems unreasonable to deny *Institutiones oratoriae* any philosophical significance, as Nicolini did. Nicolini's standpoint may have been influenced by his friend, Benedetto Croce, who had discarded the philosophical value of Vico's *Institutiones oratoriae* already in 1909.[8] This important work of Vico was to a large extent neglected until Guiliano Crifò edited it in 1989 in an unabridged and critical edition.[9]

The first chapter of my book contains a description of Peregrini's interpretation of Aristotle's theory of style and especially of acute remarks. In this chapter I shall also outline Peregrini's position towards the literary aesthetics of his time. Peregrini was a theoretician to whom Vico openly referred in his rhetoric, *Institutiones oratoriae*, but also a theoretician whom he rejected in his final definition of ingenuity and metaphorical reasoning. This aspect will be dealt with in the second chapter. In the third chapter I shall explain the epistemological and methodological consequences of Vico's stance towards Peregrini. Finally, the fourth chapter treats Vico's refusal of Descartes—a refusal which turns out to be inspired by Vico's background, the aesthetics and epistemology of literary mannerism.

Notes

1   Vico, *Vita*, *Opere* V, pp. 3-8, 20, 24, 44-46.
2   One important exception is the study of Michael Mooney, *Vico in the Tradition of Rhetoric*, to which I am indebted.
3   Nicolini's note to Vico's *Institutiones oratoriae*, *Opere* VIII, pp. 220, 222.
4   Vico, *Vita*, *Opere* V, pp. 89–93.
5   Nicolini's note to *Institutiones oratoriae*, in Vico, *Opere* VIII, p. 229.
6   *Ibid.*, p. 223.
7   *Ibid.*, pp. 182–190.
8   Benedetto Croce, *Estetica come scienza dell'espressione e linguistica generale*, p. 260: "Conosceva [Vico] per filo e per segno i trattatisti dell'acutezza e del concettare; giacché, in un arido manuale rettorico, scritto a uso della sua scuola, nel quale invano si cercarebbe un'ombra di pensiero vichiano, cita Paolo Beni, il Peregrini, lo Sforza–Palavicino, il marchese Orsi."
9   G. Vico, *Institutiones oratoriae*. Ed. G. Crifò. Naples: Istituto Suor Orsola Benincasa, 1989. An English translation of Crifò's edition has turned out recently: G. Vico, *The Art of Rhetoric ('Institutiones oratoriae', 1711-1741)*. Trans. and ed. Giorgio A. Pinton and Arthur W. Shippe. In *Value Inquiry Book Series*, nr. 37. Amsterdam and Atlanta: Rodopi, 1996.

Chapter One

Peregrini on Rhetoric

Matteo Peregrini published in 1639 *Delle acutezze, che altrimenti spiriti, vivezze e concetti volgarmente si appellano*, in the following pages abbreviated to *Delle acutezze*. Vico, in his *Institutiones oratoriae*, made important references to this book of Peregrini, but not to his other book, *I fonti dell'ingegno ridotti ad arte* (The Sources of Ingenuity According to a Method), of 1650. Consequently, I shall only deal with the passages from *Delle acutezze*, which were important in relation to Vico's concept of ingenuity.

The alleged purpose of *Delle acutezze* was to oppose a depraved use of rhetoric which took place among contemporary men of letters. Peregrini states:

> Among the depravities which have recently been sneaking in, contaminating common speech, indiscreet affectedness of *acutezze*,[1] conceit or lively wit seems to exceed all the other ones. This is a kind of embellishment more flattering and

tickling than any other one, and therefore it is very powerful in
leading to great disappointments the minds of those who are
infatuated by it. Flattery has always been a mischievous
adviser, and the escort of pleasure, when the mighty bridle of
sound judgement does not rein it in, will always be an escort
of little faith. For this reason people nowadays get carried
away, right to the point where they impudently deliver the
most obvious lies. And one may very well say in the words of
Quintilian about some of these otherwise very kind spirits, that
"perverseness of judgement leads to the most detestable
absurdities".[2]

Peregrini writes that his contemporaries use *acutezza* as a key–concept
within rhetoric, and that *acutezza* is used to amuse by style in an affected
way. This hedonistic element was part of classical rhetoric, as *delectatio*,
but not all of it; according to Cicero a rhetorician should also be able to
move, *movere*, and instruct, *docere*.[3]

Peregrini's criticism is still remarkable. On one hand he
describes the overwhelming and depraved use of *acutezze* as
embellishment, *artificio*, thus lamenting that rhetoric has been reduced to
elocutio, ornamentation; on the other hand, he intends to present an idea
of rhetoric in which the concept *acutezza*, a stylistic concept itself, has a
basic role. In other words, he does not regard the reduction of rhetoric to
elocutio as a decay; but the way in which *elocutio*, style, is conceived.

Even though Peregrini claims that he bases his criticism on
Aristotle's *Rhetoric*, and even though he uses central definitions of acute
remarks and the ability to use metaphors from this book of Aristotle, he
still conceives of rhetoric in a radically different way than Aristotle did.
According to Aristotle, the logical argument is the most important
element in rhetoric.[4] All this is treated in the first and second book of his
Rhetoric. The style by which the argument is delivered, is treated in the
third book, and it is regarded as secondary. Peregrini, however, bases his
idea of rhetoric on the third book of Aristotle's *Rhetoric*, and not even all
of it, only those lines which treat acute remarks, *ta asteia*. So, while
Aristotle regards rhetoric as a theory of argumentation, Peregrini regards
rhetoric as a theory of style. Before dealing with Peregrini's *Delle
acutezze*, it may be useful to outline Aristotle's scattered remarks on
style and its cognitive aspects, someting which Peregrini is very alert to.

1. Aristotle on Style

Aristotle's *Poetics* was rediscovered in the fifteenth century and edited by Giorgio Valla (?–1499) in a Latin translation in 1498. In the sixteenth century the *Poetics* was translated and published several times in Latin, Greek and the vernacular. It was commented on by many scholars and attracted a significant interest throughout the sixteenth century. The rediscovery and interest affected the humanists' idea about the unity of form and content, which was echoed in the theory of literary mannerism in the seventeenth century.[5]

As I have pointed out, rhetoric was conceived of as *elocutio* or *forma ornata* among mannerist theoreticians, also Peregrini, and they strove to synthesise Aristotle's *Poetics* with his *Rhetoric* in order to elaborate a theory wherein style is conceived of as more than pure ornamentation, extrinsic to thought, but as vital to thought itself. What interested these theoreticians in these books of Aristotle was only the passages which were useful to the aesthetic discussion of their epoch: If rhetoric is reduced to *elocutio*, then how is it possible to avoid rhetoric becoming hedonistic and without epistemological content? The problem was highly relevant to mannerist literature, since rhetoric served as its theoretical foundation.[6]

Against this background, mannerist theoreticians synthesised passages from the two books of Aristotle which treat style and its cognitive significance: the third book of his *Rhetoric*, in particular chapter eleven and twelve; and chapter nineteen to twenty–one in his *Poetics*. I shall now move on to explain Aristotle's idea about style in a systematic and synthesised manner, as it appears in these passages from his *Poetics* and *Rhetoric*. But I must underline that I do so without claiming that this synthesis is stated explicitly by Aristotle, Peregrini or any of the other mannerists; I present it simply because it makes sense in relation to Peregrini's and Vico's idea of style.[7] I shall focus on three aspects of style: metaphors and similes; the ability to produce these; and acute or witty remarks.

Aristotle's theory concerning metaphor is based upon his theory of the noun, which he defines as a compound of sound with a meaning.[8] In the logical works of Aristotle the noun is assigned an important position from a semantic and ontological point of view: in his semantics, the noun is incorporated into a correspondence theory of truth; and in his ontology, the noun corresponds to various ontological classes—genera, species and individuals. These two aspects are presupposed in Aristotle's theory on metaphor. He states:

> Metaphor is the application of a strange term either transferred
> from the genus and applied to the species or from the species
> and applied to the genus, or from one species to another or else
> by analogy.[9]

In essence, metaphor is a semantic transformation, which can take place in those four ways. He offers the following examples: from genus to species, "here *stands* my ship", where the anchoring is a species of standing, which is regarded as a genus; from species to genus, "indeed *ten thousand* noble things Odysseus did", where ten thousand is a species substituting "many", which is a genus; from species to species, "*drawing off* his life with the bronze", and "*severing* with the tireless bronze", where "drawing off" is used for "severing", and "severing" for "drawing off", both being species of "removing"; finally, metaphor by analogy; when B is to A as D is to C, then these relations can be formulated analogically by saying D instead of B, and B instead of D. Aristotle gives an example:

A: Dionysus
B: Drinking bowl
C: Ares
D: Shield

The relation between these four nouns, known from Greek mythology, can be expressed like this:

$$\frac{\text{Drinking bowl (B)}}{\text{Dionysus (A)}} = \frac{\text{Shield (D)}}{\text{Ares (C)}}$$

This relation is represented as we know it from Greek mythology—yet no semantic transformation is involved. But that will happened if the relation is expressed through metaphor by analogy:

$$\frac{\text{Shield (D)}}{\text{Dionysus (A)}} = \frac{\text{Drinking bowl (B)}}{\text{Ares (C)}}$$

This metaphor by analogy says that the drinking bowl is "the shield of Ares", and that the shield is "the drinking bowl of Dionysus".[10]

In his *Rhetoric* Aristotle refers to these four types of metaphor, mentioned in the *Poetics*,[11] but he also develops a fifth type, the simile, from metaphor by analogy.[12] For instance, if we say about Achilles that he "rushed away like a lion", then we are using a simile by which something is said to be like something else. But if we said, "the lion rushed away", and it is implicit that "lion" refers to the person Achilles, then we are using a metaphor by analogy, expressing that they are both courageous. These two examples illustrate the difference between metaphor, a word in transferred meaning, and simile, in which something is said to be like something else. In both examples a qualitative similarity is recognised (both the lion and Achilles are courageous); in the simile this is stated explicitly, but not in the metaphor, where a further step has been taken by transferring a name from one thing ("lion" about the lion), to another thing (Achilles), which shares a property with the first thing (i.e. courageousness). In brief, in metaphor a semantic transformation is added.

These definitions of metaphor and simile relate to the linguistic expression. But Aristotle also comments on the epistemological operation producing such rhetorical figures. Immediately after the definition of metaphor, he says about the ability to use metaphors:

> ...by far the greatest thing is the use of metaphor. That alone cannot be learnt; it is the token of ingenuity. For the right use of metaphor means an eye for resemblance.[13]

To use metaphors is to "see the like", that is, to comprehend a (qualitative) identity between (numerically) different things. The ability to recognise such a resemblance is particular to poets and philosophers.[14]

Although Aristotle regards rhetoric and poetics as teachable methods for producing speeches and fiction, he holds that the ability to see likeness, an important precondition for the creation of speeches and fiction, cannot be taught.

In Aristotle's *Rhetoric,* the ability to see similarities is also important in relation to the use of acute or witty sayings, *asteia*.[15] Contrary to the rhetorical figures mentioned in the *Poetics*, which are used within literature, *asteion* is a kind of saying which we find within oral communication. Aristotle's reflections upon the ability to produce acute or witty remarks became crucial in the rhetorical theories developed by Tesauro and Peregrini, since these reflections of Aristotle were useful in their effort to reconcile rhetoric, understood as *elocutio* and exclusively concerned with style, with a pedagogical content.

According to Aristotle, *asteion* is an expression with condensed meaning, by which the speaker teaches or instructs the audience rapidly. In the case of acute sayings, this instruction is undertaken through a surprising comparison, thus involving the ability to see similarities between different things. Furthermore, it is pleasing to be taught or instructed—the faster, the more pleasing. Metaphors and similes possess this pedagogical feature, so they are considered as acute sayings. If the use of metaphor, in accordance with the definition stated above, is the use of a noun with a foreign meaning, then the speaker's use of metaphor will teach the audience something new about the subject matter to which the noun is transferred; therefore, Aristotle holds, metaphors are pleasing. Not only metaphors, but also similes are providing new knowledge by their identifications. Still, metaphor by analogy is the most popular one because of its condensed form, which brings about a more rapid instruction than any other kind of metaphor. Metaphor by analogy is more popular than the simile for the same reason; in a simile everything is unfolded and nothing is left implicit, which is why it is longer and instructs less rapidly. Likewise, the enthymeme, a syllogism with an implicit premis, is faster in its instruction than a complete syllogism.[16]

Metaphor is a suitable form of expression of acute remarks because of its basic substitution of nouns' normal meaning with a foreign meaning, but certainly also because of its typical figurative character. In fact, Aristotle claims that figuretiveness is the criterion for the form of expression of acute remarks; it must be a form of expression which "puts things before the eye".[17] Aristotle's emphasis upon the role of mental images in relation to acute remarks, as they are described in his *Rhetoric*, has some relation to the ability to see similarities, so central in the use of metaphors and described in his *Poetics;* in both instances mental images play a vital role in reasoning. Furthermore, as I have already said, the poet and the speaker on one hand, and the philosopher on the other hand, share a capacity to discover similarity between different things; this capacity is central in the use of *asteia.*[18]

In the concept *asteion, acutezza* in Italian, we find the starting point for the literary mannerism to reconcile a hedonistic element at one side, *delectare*, and a pedagogical on the other side, *docere*, and that is one of the main reasons why acuteness turns out to be an important concept during this epoch. In mannerism, Aristotle's thoughts on *asteion* were further elaborated, from a mere theory on the popularity of the sayings to a theory concerning the epistemological potential. In what follows I shall deal with Peregrini's treatment of these thoughts.

2. '*Acutezza*'

Peregrini's purpose with *Delle acutezze* is to establish a criterion to distinguish empty wordplays from pointed remarks. Before Peregrini carries out this distinction, he defines *acutezza* in an original manner:

> In order to present more clearly what has been said in the preceding chapter, and to investigate the nature of the wondrous *acutezze* in depth, I shall proceed as follows. In a sentence there is nothing but words, signified objects and their mutual connection. The words as well as the objects or things, which are considered separately, are sheer matter: therefore, *acutezza* is necessarily concerned with the connection. This can apply to the relation between words, between things and words, or between things; and in each case the connection may be with or without style. When the connection is natural or causal or otherwise without artifice, it cannot equally show any problem belonging to our examination, because it is presupposed that an *acutezza* is something stylish. Since the artifice must produce something wondrous, it must not be

ordinary, but rather, remarkably rare. And since it must shape
an object which is extremely delightful for the mind to look at,
its rarity and impressiveness will result from the ability to
make a very decorous order to appear between the parts which
are joined with style in the sentence...Therefore, in the
connection, which comes from style, both in regard to things
and to words, which is to be considered here, the strength must
depend entirely on the mutual order of the parts.[19]

Essentially, Peregrini describes *acutezza* as the relation of parts in a
sentence; this relation is more important than the subject matter. The
point of departure for this definition of *acutezza* is Aristotle's
corresponding concept, *asteion*, but Peregrini differs from Aristotle in
his definition: Aristotle's notion *asteion* signifies a remark which
instructs rapidly because of its condensed form. Consequently, metaphor
and metaphor by analogy are forms of expression suitable for acute
remarks. And metaphor is, as said, defined as a successful substitution of
a normally used noun with a foreign noun. So, to Aristotle *asteion* is
expressed in a single word, the one in transferred meaning; but Peregrini
defines *acutezza* as the relation of the parts in the sentence, of which the
word in transferred meaning is part. Surely, this point was also implied
in Aristotle's definition of metaphor—especially metaphor by analogy
which requires an eye for the relation between several parts—but in his
final definition of metaphor and *asteion* the substitution was stressed.
Peregrini's reformulating of *acutezza* implies a break with the idea of
Aristotle and of rhetoric as *elocutio*, in which style is conceived as
ornamentation undertaken through metaphors, that is, substituted words:
since *acutezza* concerns the relation of parts in a sentence, including
words in transferred meaning, *acutezza* reveals a new perspective from
which the single parts are seen. In brief, Peregrini assigns *acutezza* a
predicative function, while Aristotle assigns *asteion* a substituting
function.

In the quotation above, it is said that the parts of *acutezza* can
concern "the relation between words, between things and words, or
between things". Here "words", *parole*, must be understood as tangible
sounds, while "things" must mean ideas about something.[20] In the case
of "words", related with "mutual order" through the artifice, we may

recognise a reminiscence of the humanist Ermolao Barbaro (1453–1493) and his concept *concinnitas*, the stylistic rounding of the words in a sentence. Peregrini, however, does not mention Ermolao Barbaro as his source, but Cicero.[21] Peregrini distinguishes between these three sorts of relations in a sentence, in order to separate two kinds of *acutezza*; *acutezza leggiadria*, elegant acuteness, which only concerns the relation of the words as harmonious sounds, e.g. rhyme. This is the kind of *acutezza* which Peregrini condemns in the first quotation above, since it is purely verbal. He may be aiming at the poet Giambattista Marino (1569–1625) who had defended the opposite point of view, that the popularity of the delivery and its elocution is sufficient justification.[22] This does not mean that Peregrini discards the idea of rhetoric as *elocutio*—in fact he affirms it, but in a moderate form: on one hand, he accepts that the language of eloquence and poetry must possess an aesthetic form; on the other hand, he claims that this form can be of two kinds, and that only one of them possesses a semantic content, namely *acutezza mirabile*, wondrous acuteness. *Acutezza mirabile* we find in sentences where the relation of the artifice regards connections between "words and things" or between "things". Of course, this relation may well be harmonious as in *acutezza leggiadria*, but there must exist a semantic content too. About this kind of *acutezza* Peregrini says:

> The stylish connection of words with things takes place every time the sound or the elocution is judiciously transported from its normal meaning to a foreign one. In this case, yet more things are tacitly related to things, because the thing newly signified will tacitly be connected to that thing which is signified normally—not only because of the term being made common, but also for the reason which made this association possible. This stylish connection can—because of the quality of the words and itself—reach the point where it produces such a rare harmoniousness, that it obviously reveals itself as stemming from a special kind of dexterity.[23]

This description of wondrous acuteness may seem obscure. I have already explained this form of *acutezza* as a sentence containing a relation between things, or ideas; but in this quotation Peregrini claims that the relating of ideas takes place through sounds, *voce*, or elocution, *locuzione*. One might have expected that the epistemological operation, to relate one idea with another, simply requires the ability to know and to relate the respective ideas, directly; but Peregrini states that the ability to relate ideas depends upon the ability to grasp and relate similarities in the appearance of the words or sounds representing these ideas. Our ideas are given through language, and if we want to relate separate ideas, it must take place through a discovery of similarities in the tangible material of the language expressing those ideas. According to Peregrini, ingenuity is capable of relating ideas through such phonetic similarities and dissimilarities. He characterises this capacity as *accortezza*, swiftness or adroitness, particular to ingenuity.

This principle of wondrous acuteness is illustrated with an example from the biography of Roman emperors, *De vita caesarum* (Lives of the Caesars), written by the Latin author Suetonius (70–140 AD). Here we find a biography of the emperor Augustus (63 BC–14 AD). Suetonius relates that Augustus had been writing on a tragedy, which he had destroyed because of his poor talent for literary work. When Augustus was asked by friends what had happened to "his Ajax", i.e. his tragedy, he replied that "Aiacem suum in spongiam incubisse" (his Ajax had fallen on his sponge); Augustus had erased his tragedy.[24] In order to understand this reply, it is necessary to know the literary figure Ajax as he is portrayed in Greek mythology: In Homer's *Iliad* he was one of the heroes fighting with the Greeks in the Trojan War. It is related, outside the *Iliad*, that when Achilles, by far the greatest hero among the Greeks, was killed, Odysseus and Ajax were arguing about who should inherit the weapons of Achilles as a mark of honour. The leaders on the Greek side decided to hand over the weapons to Odysseus. Ajax was deeply offended and committed suicide by throwing himself against his own sword. Peregrini comments on the quotation by Suetonius and its allusion to Ajax' death: that in Italian, sword is called "spada", which, regarding its sound, is similar to the Latin word for sponge, "spongia". The sword and the sponge are both means to "erase"; the sponge erases something written; the sword is used to kill. By using the word "spongia" together with the literary figure Ajax, Suetonius makes the reader associate his Ajax, the tragedy written by Augustus, with the Greek hero Ajax who committed suicide. The example indicates how phonetic similarities provide the semantic transformation, taking place in *acutezza mirabile*.

In Peregrini's description of *acutezza mirabile* we find a formulation which refers to Aristotle's definition of metaphor: "the stylistic connection of words with things takes place every time the sound or the elocution is judiciously transported from its normal meaning to a foreign one." This formulation is close to Aristotle's definition of metaphor as a transference of a noun from its native meaning to a foreign one. Nevertheless, they differ radically in their understanding of metaphor: Peregrini does not take over Aristotle's emphasis upon metaphor as a substitution of one noun with another, but underlines the epistemological process preceding the substitution; a discovery of similarities between subject matters, which takes place through a discovery of phonetic similarities between the words expressing these matters. To Aristotle, the similarity between several subject matters is something given, but not according to Peregrini, who insists that such an identification must be proceeded by the association which arises from similarities between words, as tangible material. This crucial difference in the conception of metaphor is obvious in their use of examples: In Aristotle's example of metaphor by analogy, it is not asked how the relations between the words—Dionysus, the drinking bowl, Ares and the shield—are established; Aristotle simply presupposes that such relations exist. To Aristotle metaphor signifies a word in a transferred meaning, and this word has, as such, a fixed meaning; to Peregrini, on the other hand, the creation of a metaphor is an invention and articulation of a new and original meaning.[25]

As I have already pointed out, Peregrini also differs from Aristotle in his basic definition of *acutezza*, corresponding to Aristotle's notion *asteion*: *acutezza* is not simply a sentence in which a word is transferred from its normal meaning to a foreign one, but the relation of the words in the whole sentence. Consequently, in the case of *acutezza mirabile*, a new perspective on reality is created through the relation between words; "things" are related to other "things" through the word in transferred meaning and its phonetic relation to other words. In practise, this opening of a new perspective appears as a dazzling evasion of the semantic structure particular to the linguistic community in which the *acutezza mirabile* is advanced. Peregrini demands that such a sentence must be rare and remote from the normal way of using the words in question. Unfortunately, this demand has often been misunderstood as a prohibition against treating something common and everyday; as a demand only to advance incomprehensible and dazzling remarks. But that is wrong. The speaker must know the historical reality and the common usage of language, especially the phonetic and semantic aspects of the concrete language; without this knowledge the speaker will fail to create *acutezza mirabile*. In this sense one might say that *sensus communis* is of utmost importance.

So much for *acutezza leggiadria*, relating words, and *acutezza mirabile*, relating things through words. A third kind of relation, direct relations between things, remains. In a remark of the kind *acutezza leggiadria* there is no semantic counterpart to the tangible order between the signs, but in *acutezza mirabile* we do find such a semantic counterpart too. The epistemological capacity to create new and surprising perspectives through *acutezze mirabili* is particular to ingenuity, and Peregrini underlines this in relation to an *acutezza mirabile* advanced by Cato:

> This happened [*acutezza mirabile*] when Cato, speaking about one who said, after he had used up most of his property in gluttony and finally lost his last house in a fire: "I have done 'sacrifice for the road.'"[26] This was the expression of a sacrifice in which, after having dined well, all the leftovers from supper were burnt, according to habit and rite of religion. The invention of such a befitting comparison through which the word was conveyed from its normal meaning to its new meaning, made such ingenious adroitness shine in the sentence as to make Cato ever since remarkably wondrous.[27]

Having reached this point, Peregrini has fulfilled the ambition he set out at the beginning, to lay down a criterion to distinguish between two kinds *acutezza*, one deprived of semantic content, *acutezza leggiadria*, and another with such a content, *acutezza mirabile*, and he has pointed out the vital role of ingenuity in the creation of *acutezza mirabile*. But he goes on to claim that the interrelating of ideas through the artifice of *acutezza*, worked out by ingenuity, is not the only way to connect ideas; logic is another discipline teaching how to relate ideas, and he examines the role of stylistic sensibility, particular to ingenuity, within this discipline.

3. Ingenuity

Peregrini calls a relation between ideas an "intelligible relation", which he divides into two kinds: two ideas can be related without any means. This is the case when a noun is predicated with an adjective. Such a mental operation is the "second operation of the intellect". Or the intelligible relation between two ideas can be mediated by a third idea. In that case we are dealing with a logical inference, the "third operation of the intellect". Among logicians this inference takes place through the syllogism, among rhetoricians through the enthymeme.[28]

The intellect's relating of two nouns by a third takes place according to the rules of logic—as in the case of the syllogism and that of the enthymeme. The purpose is simply to teach. In this purely informative way of speaking, undertaken through syllogisms and enthymemes without any pleasing artifice, no new and ingenious perspective is advanced:

> This kind of connection can, nevertheless, produce pleasure depending on the matter which it uses, owing to the great sagacity of the intellect such as is rarely seen in the invention of the middle term, and also owing to the quality of the things which it teaches, but not because it opens any ingenious perspective. Here the intellect does not really create, but only unveils and presents. Therefore, the operation of the intellect is not the most important object in the awareness of the audience or the reader, but the truth demonstrated alone is the object that matters.[29]

The operation of the intellect is nothing but an explication of a perspective already laid down. Peregrini is not specific about the perspective to which he refers, but since he is talking about logic here, one might think that he is referring to the perspective on reality found in the ontological scheme of the Aristotelians, a scheme which concerns the order between genera and species and individuals; the terms of logic corresponds neatly to those classes, and the form of the syllogistic reasoning, an inference from universal to individual, is likewise in accordance with it. This description of Aristotelian logic as powerless and without ability to discover new knowledge, might be an echo of the criticism raised by some of the humanists.

Against this background, Peregrini makes a distinction between intellect and ingenuity, and in the following passage he makes a comparison between the pedagogical role of the intellect and the embellishing and hedonistic role of ingenuity:

> Indeed, truth has a very delightful face; nevertheless, it is a delight different from the kind which I am intending to pinpoint here. A proposition by Euclid delights you if your mind is able to grasp it, but such a delight is different from the one which you may experience when hearing an ingenious epigram by Martial. In brief, style has its role not only or principally in discovering beautiful things, but also in devising them; and the object of the plausible in our enquiry does not belong to the intellect, which only seeks truth and knowledge of things, but, rather, to ingenuity, which both in operating and as well in its enjoyment has as its object not so much truth, as beauty.[30]

In this passage, Peregrini strongly contrasts the role of each capacity, thus presenting the intellect as a cognitive faculty searching for truth, and ingenuity as a non–cognitive faculty exclusively occupied with beauty. Is this brief characteristic of ingenuity to be believed? If so, then the development from Peregrini to Vico becomes more significant, since Vico claims that ingenuity is a cognitive faculty. But I think that a more sustainable interpretation is that Peregrini is ambiguous, at best: Before the sharp separation between the cognitive intellect and the non–cognitive ingenuity, he discerned two forms of *acutezza*, claiming that through the artifice of *acutezza mirabile* a new perspective is opened towards reality; would it be unfair to say that ingenuity carries out a cognitive operation in this manner? No. Ingenuity is confined to a purely aesthetic function in its invention of a suitable embellishment, but in the case of *acutezza mirabile*, the "suitable" is not exclusively suitable from an aesthetic point of view, but indeed also from a semantic point of view.[31]

The quotation above not only suggests a partition between intellect and ingenuity, but also, parallel with these two faculties, a partition between logic and rhetoric: Rhetoric ("the plausible in our enquiry") is treating the question how ingenuity creates something beautiful, *il bello*. The purpose of the creation is to please the speaker or the audience, that is, *delectatio*. According to Peregrini, the scope of rhetoric is not, as Cicero said, to put forward an argument in the speech, but to embellish the speech. Logic, on the other hand, guides the intellect in its search for truth, *il vero*, wherefore it can be ascribed another scope than rhetoric, namely to teach, *docere*. The intellect is regarded as important in science, i.e. the apodictic sciences, in which a high degree of certainty can be found; ingenuity, as Peregrini said above, works in rhetoric as far as it is applied within the probable sciences, that is, in relation to ethics and social issues, in which the matter is less certain and allows for a less rigid argumentation.[32]

Compared with classical rhetoric, we find remarkable correspondences and differences in Peregrini's conception of rhetoric and ingenuity. In classical rhetoric the task of ingenuity is to invent or discover the middle term of the syllogism, or enthymeme; this part is called invention, *inventio*.[33] In the idea of rhetoric which Peregrini suggests here, this classical *inventio*, worked out by the intellect as a logical operation, is discarded as a real *inventio*; it is only seen as a way to present subject matters from a perspective already established. But ingenuity, Peregrini claims, is capable of a true *inventio*, and this *inventio* does not take place through logical discernment, but through an aesthetic one, that is, through a linguistic sensibility and creativity.

Consequently, no syllogism involves ingenuity. Unless in the case of the enthymeme, a syllogism in abbreviated form, when it is embellished by an artifice. In that case, Peregrini holds, *acutezza* may turn out, and he describes it like this:

> Therefore, the rarity of the invention in the enthymematic connection which matters here, should not so much be explained by the finding of a perfect junction of a middle term with the mediated terms,[34] as by the creation of a decorous,

very rare and outstanding form of expression. When the
joining middle term and the mediated terms are represented in
their natural order, nothing rare can be created; and when
artifice is completely absent, you cannot hope for anything but
a good and clear syllogistic connection. And this will satisfy
the intellect, but will not satisfy ingenuity at all. It is therefore
necessary that either the middle terms or the mediated terms,
or both, are well–devised, and, as the rhetorician would say,
figurati [i.e. forming a rhetorical figure]. And since the art
does not have any special, certain and easy rules such as may
represent the above said parts with such rarity that from it a
very gracious and befitting form of expression may arise, the
whole business depends on the power of ingenuity, which
cannot be wondrous unless by operating in an excellent way
where there are no specific rules for operating well. When the
figured connection succeeds in forming a very rare and
befitting form of expression between the connected parts, so
that the force of ingenuity shows itself as the main object of
marvellousness in this act, we shall have the wondrous
acutezza.[35]

Such an embellished enthymeme is an acute sentence, *detto acuto*.[36]
Peregrini refers explicitly to Aristotle when describing ingenuity which
creates such an artifice: "He also said that the ability to see
correspondences between different things is characteristic of a clever
mind, and that devising the middle term to connect different things in a
suitable way is nothing but finding such suitability in the expression."[37]
Peregrini uses this statement as a point of departure for his own
definition of ingenuity. In Aristotle, the skill of the intellect is defined by
its ability to discover a middle term in a syllogism.[38] Peregrini defines
the skill of ingenuity analogically:

> From this it becomes possible to understand the nature of the
> particular skill of ingenuity, by which the *acutezza* is created.
> Because, just as Aristotle defined the skill of the intellect as a
> promptness to find successfully the middle term to make the
> demonstration, so we shall be able to define the skill of
> ingenuity relative to our discussion as a successful invention
> of a middle term connecting figuratively different things in a
> saying with marvellous aptness.[39]

The full title of Peregrini's book is *Delle acutezze, che altrimenti spiriti, vivezze e concetti volgarmente si appellano.* What he calls *spiriti, vivezze e concetti*—jokes, acute remarks and aphorisms—refer to the stylistic sensibility and mode of reasoning, very central to the creation of acute sayings.[40] With this theory Peregrini was one of the first in Italy who presented a theory on *il concettismo,* the symbolic accumulation of ideas through literary style, named literary mannerism in this book. In the following chapter we shall see how Vico picked up some of these ideas and presented them in his theory of rhetoric.

Notes

1   *Acutezza* may refer to a sentence (acute saying) or to a cognitive ability (acuteness).

2   Peregrini, *Delle acutezze*, p. 113: "Tra le corruttele che a contaminar la facondia prosaica novellamente serpeggiano, l'indiscreta affettazione delle acutezze, concetti o spiriti, sopra tutte l'altre peravventura si avanza. Questo è un genere d'abbellimento più di tutti quanti se n'abbia l'arte lusinghiero e solleticante, e però molto possente a traer gli animi d'esso invaghiti a grandissimi trasviamenti. La lusinga fu sempre un consigliere malvagio, e la scorta del diletto, dove poderosa briglia di buon giudicio nol freni, fia sempre scorta poco fedele. A cagione di ciò si trasanda tanto oggidì per questa traccia, che si viene a sfacciatamente dare in apertissime ciurmerie; e può ben con le parole di Quintiliano dirsi d'alcuni altrimenti gentilissimi spiriti che 'pravis ingeniis ad foedissima usque ludibria labuntur'."

3   Cicero, *De optimo genere oratorum* 1.3.

4   Aristotle, *Rhetoric* 1354.

5   Garin, *L'umanesimo italiano*, p. 186.

6   See Cesare: "La filosofia dell'ingegno e dell'acutezza di Matteo Pellegrini e il suo legame con la retorica di Giambattista Vico," p. 158; Morpurgo–Tagliabue, *Anatomia del barocco*, pp. 16ff.

7   My sources in the following pages about Aristotle's *Poetics* and *Rhetoric* are indebted to Anna Maria Contini's lectures on Tesauro, held at the university of Bologna, 1993–1994.

8   Aristotle, *Poetics* 1457a.

9   *Ibid.*, 1457b.

10 *Ibid.*

11 Aristotle, *Rhetoric* 1411a.

12 *Ibid.*, 1406b; 1412b–1413a.

13 Aristotle, *Poetics* 1459a.

14 *Ibid.*, *Rhetoric* 1412a.

15 *Ibid.*, 1410b. See Andrea Battistini, "Acutezza," B1.

16 Aristotle, *Rhetoric* 1410b–1411a.

17 *Ibid.*, 1411b.

18 *Ibid.*, 1412a. See Morpurgo–Tagliabue, *Anatomia del barocco*, pp. 29–34.

19 Peregrini, *Delle acutezze*, p. 118: "Per far comparir più chiaro quanto nel capo precedente si è detto, e per internamente la nautra dell'acutezze mirabili investigare, io discorro in questa maniera. In un detto non è altro che parole, obbietti significati e loro vicendevole collegamento. Le parole, sì come anche gli obbietti o cose appartatamente considerate, sono pura materia: dunque l'accutezza si regge necessariamente dal legamento. Questo può considerarsi tra parole e parole, tra cose e parole, tra cose e cose; e in ciascuna di queste maniere può esser artificioso e anco essere senza artificio. Quando sia naturale o casuale o altrimenti senza artificio, non può parimente rilevar punto al proposto nostro, perché l'acutezza per cosa artificiosa si è presupposta. L'artificio, perché ha da partorir il mirabile, non dovrà essere comunale, ma grandemente raro; e perché ha da formar obbietto di vista all'animo fortemente dilettevole, la sua rarità e virtù si speigherà nel far comparire una molto vicendevole acconcezza tra le parti nel detto

artificiosamente legate. ...Dunque nell'artificioso legamento, sia di cose o parole, che qui viene a considerarsi, il pregio tutto dipenderà dalla vicendevole loro acconcezza."

20 See Lange, *Theoretiker des literarischen Manierismus,* p. 124.

21 Peregrini quotes Cicero in *Delle acutezze,* p. 119: "concinnitate quandam et constructione verborum." The quotation refers to Cicero, *Orator* 49.164. Concerning the term "concinnitas", see Lausberg, *Handbuch der literarischen Rhetorik,* § 458. Peregrin's occupation with literary style may be an echo of the discussion of style in the Italian Renaissance: See Kraye, "Philologists and Philosophers."

22 Franco Croce, "Le poetiche del barocco in Italia," p. 550.

23 Peregrini, *Delle acutezze*, p. 120: "Il legamento artificoso delle parole con le cose accade ogni volta che la voce o la locuzione sia giudiciosamente trasportata dal suo nativo significato ad un alieno. In questo caso vengono tacitamente ancora legate cose con cose, perché la cosa nuovamente significata viene tacitamente a legarsi con quella che nativamente suole significarsi, non solo per la voce fatta comune, ma insieme per quella ragione che ha fatto luogo a simile comunanza. Questo artificioso legamento può, per la qualità de' termini e per la propria, avanzarsi a partorir tale rarità d'acconcezza, che parto di speciale destrezza ancor egli palesemente si mostri."

24 Peregrini, *Delle acutezze*, p. 120. From Suetonius, *Augustus* 85.2.

25 See Cesare, "La filosofia dell'ingegno e dell'acutezza di Matteo Pellegrini e il suo legame con la retorica di Giambattista Vico," p. 163.

26 Macrobius, *Saturnalia* 2.2.4: "Sacrifice for the road": "propter viam".

27 Peregrini, *Delle acutezze,* p. 120: "Così avvenne quando Catone, parlando d'uno che, dopo aver consumato le sostanze in ghiottornie, per incendio finalmente perdette una casa che sola gli era rimasta, disse: 'Ha fatto il *propter viam.*' Questo era il nome d'un sacrificio nel quale, dopo l'aver ben mangiato, per costume e rito di religione si abbrugiavano tutti gli avanzi. Il trovar la proporzione tanto campeggiante, mediante la quale fu luogo al trasportar la parola molto acconciamente dal proprio significato all'alieno, fe' splendere nel detto tale accortezza d'ingegno, ch'egli restò notabilmente ammirabile."

28 *Ibid.*, pp. 121f.

29 *Ibid*, p. 122: "Può nondimeno a cagione della materia soggetta recar diletto per la molta accortezza dell'intelletto, che nell'invenzione del mezzo raramente in esso faccia vedersi, e anco per la qualità delle cose in esso imparate, ma non già perché faccia oggetto di prospettiva ingegnosa. L'intelletto qui non forma veramente, ma solo discopre e porge. Però l'opera sua non si rende principal oggetto dell'animo altrui, ma oggetto è la sola verità dimostrata."

30 *Ibid.*, p. 122: "Ella veramente ha faccia dilettevolissima; nulladimeno in genere di diletto differente a quello che qui si cerca. Diletta una proposizione d'Euclide quando se ne acquista l'intelligenza, ma simil diletto è molto differente da quello che si provi nell'udir un ingegnoso epigramma di Marziale. In somma, l'artificio ha luogo solamente o principalmente non già nel trovar cose belle, ma nel farle; e l'oggetto del plausibile a nostro proposito non s'appartiene all'intelletto, che solo cerca la verità e scienza delle cose, ma sì bene all'ingegno, il quale tanto nell'operare quanto nel compiacersi ha per oggetto non tanto il vero quanto il bello."

31 Cf. Lange, *Theoretiker des literarischen Manierismus,* p. 137; Cesare, "La filosofia dell'ingegno e dell'acutezza di Matteo Pellegrini e il suo legame con la retorica di Giambattista Vico," pp. 166ff.

32 See Aristotle, *Nicmachean Ethics* 1140a–1141a.

33 Cicero, *Topica* 1.2.

34 With the expressions "middle term" and "mediated terms" Peregrini refers to the syllogism: "mediated terms" are the nouns or subjects presented in the two premisses of the syllogism; "middle term" is the predicate which unites these two nouns or subjects and makes a conclusion possible.

35 Peregrini, *Delle acutezze*, pp. 122f: "Dunque la rarità dell'artificio nel legamento entimematico al nostro fine non si spiega tanto nel trovare una perfetta congiunzione del mezzo con gli estremi, quanto nel formare una vicendevole, molto rara e campeggiante acconcezza. Dove il mezzo congiugnente e le cose congiunte stiano nella natural condizion loro, non si può formar cosa alcuna di raro; e mancando affatto l'artificio, altro di pregio non può sperarsi che una buona e chiara connnessione sillogistica: e così all'intelletto molto sodisfare, ma non già punto all'ingegno. Egli è dunque mestiere che 'l mezzo o gli estremi o tutti sieno artificiosi e, come direbbe il retore, figurati. E perché regole speciali, certe e facili, da figurar le dette parti con tanta rarità che ne risulti una molto graziosa vicendevole acconcezza non ha l'arte, rimane tutto il campo alla virtù dell'ingegno, la quale non può mostrarsi ammirabile salvoché operando bene per eccellenza, dove per bene operare non ha regola speciale. Quando adunque il legamento figurato giugnerà a formare una tanto rara acconcezza vicendevole tra le parti collegate, che la virtù dell'ingegno facciasi in esso principale oggetto di ammirazione, averemo nel detto l'acutezza mirabile."

36 *Ibid.*, p. 124.

37 *Ibid.*, p. 125: "Disse altresì che 'l vedere le convenienze tra le cose lontane era proprio d'ingegno accorto: e 'l trovar il mezzo per legar in un detto acconciamente cose lontane non è altro che trovare simile convenienza." See Aristotle, *Rhetoric* 1410b; 1412a.

38 Aristotle, *Posterior Analytics* 89b.

39 Peregrini, *Delle acutezze*, p. 124: "Da questo ancora viene ad aprirsi via da comprendere in che consista la particolar accortezza d'ingegno genitrice del detto acuto. Perciò che, sì come Aristotele diffinì l'accortezza dell'intelletto una prestezza nel trovar felicemente il mezzo per far la dimostrazione, così noi potremo diffinir l'accortezza del'ingegno al proposto nostro un felice trovamento del mezzo per legar figuratamente in un detto con mirabile acconcezza diverse cose."

40 *Ibid.*, p. 125.

Chapter Two

Vico's 'Institutiones Oratoriae'

1. Vico on the Nature of Rhetoric

Vico refers to several of Peregrini's ideas in *Institutiones oratoriae*. But one must bear in mind that before he dealt with these ideas, he had experienced personal and cultural changes in relation to the literary culture of which Peregrini was part.

The version of *Institutiones oratoriae* which I shall deal with, is dating from 1711, when Vico was forty–three years old and had taught rhetoric for twelve years. Before receiving this lectureship he had participated in the literature of his epoch by writing poems in the mannerist style. For instance, when he was eighteen, he had followed Tesauro's advice and written poems inspired by the rose as a theme. These poems he presented to the Jesuit and poet Giacomo Lubrano. Accordingly, Vico did not begin his public career as a philosopher or as a rhetorician, but as a poet, namely with the poem *Affetti di un disperato* (Passions of a Desperate), dating from 1693. However, when Vico published his autobiography in 1725, at the age of fifty–seven, he almost apologised for his early participation in this literary movement.[1] But even before then, while still young, he realised that he had been led astray by a literary fashion which had turned into epigoni long ago, and that a counterattack had begun in France under the name neo–classicism. The Frenchman Dominique Bouhours (1628–1702) was one of the most influential neo–classicists, and his book *La mainere de bien penser dans les ouvrages d'esprit* (The Art of Critique), dating from 1691, soon found its spokesmen in Italy too. The society Arcadia, an Italian counterpart to the French neo–classicism and its criticism of the Italian literature of the seventeenth century, was founded soon after.[2] Vico was sympathetic to this new counter movement, and he became a member of Arcadia in 1710, one year before this version of his *Institutiones oratoriae*.[3] All these developments in Vico's life and in the history of Italian literature lie behind Vico's discussion of the nature of rhetoric.

Vico defines rhetoric as "a method for delivering what is suitable for the sake of persuasion".[4] This definition may originate from Aristotle, who had defined rhetoric as a method to find possible means for persuasion. Aristotle explains that the listeners can be persuaded either because of the argument of the speaker, or because of the speaker's pathos, or, because of the ethos of the listeners. He underlines, however, that the argument is the most important means. To Aristotle rhetoric is a theory of argumentation.[5]

Cicero and Quintilian had followed Aristotle's idea about rhetoric, which becomes clear in their demand to the good speaker: he must be able to instruct with his arguments, *docere*; to move with his pathos, *movere*; and to please with his style, *delectare*.[6] Vico agrees with Cicero and Quintilian.[7] It seems as if Vico returns to the elements of classical rhetoric, thus denying the development of the previous two hundred years, where the content of *docere*—*inventio* and *dispositio*— had been transferred from rhetoric to logic, and where rhetoric was left as Peregrini accepted it, an impoverished theory of *elocutio* with no other scope than to please, *delectare*. In the *Institutiones oratoriae* of Vico, the part dear to the mannerists, *delectatio*, survives, but in harmony with the classical parts *docere* and *movere*. The question is, however, whether this apparent difference should be taken at face value: Vico did not write a treatise on courtly speech, as Peregrini seems to have done; instead, Vico wrote a manual suitable for students of jurisprudence, and from that point of view it is hardly surprising that he insists upon the primacy of the logical argument, since this part must be crucial to any barrister who wants to make his case convincing.

Vico thus adheres to classical rhetoric with its traditional field, the discussion of man's historically situated social and ethical practice, *quit sit agendum*. This field he opposes tó philosophy, dealing with general arguments, *universa arguementa*.[8] In this distinction we may hear an echo of Aristotle's theory of science, in which it is a basic principle not to demand a larger degree of certainty than the object allows: in science, here roughly corresponding to Vico's term "philosophy", we are dealing with unchangeable objects about which we find certain and indisputable principles. Accordingly, a high degree of certainty can be achieved, and a correspondingly rigid manner of reflecting upon such objects is possible. Here we find the demonstrative syllogism, which deduces statements from indisputable premises and arrives at conclusions with logical necessity. But social and ethical practice cannot be regarded similarly, according to Aristotle, since this practice is variable—not unchangeable as in the field of science; therefore, this field does not allow one to argue from certain and indisputable premises, as in the field of science, and this kind of reasoning Aristotle calls dialectical reasoning. This does not mean, however, that this reasoning is arbitrary or deprived of certainty, since prudence, *phronesis*, provides the knowledge about the good life, which is useful in this kind of discussion. And rhetoric, Aristotle claims, is part of dialectical reasoning.[9] He goes on, dividing man's ethical actions into three kinds; past actions, which can be discussed in a forensic speech; actual actions, debatable in an epideictic speech; and future actions, about which we can argue in a political speech.[10] Vico follows Aristotle in this conception of the nature of rhetoric and of its specific kinds of speeches.[11] Consequently, he divides his rhetoric according to the classical model, deriving from Aristotle and known by Vico through Cicero.[12]

It may seem as if Vico were simply repeating the idea of classical rhetoric, and one might easily think that he was blind to the mannerist discussion of rhetoric. But behind the traditional understanding of rhetoric we find an original treatment of style, *elocutio*, a treatment which demonstrates that Vico had a confident relationship with mannerism and its conception of rhetoric. He describes *elocutio* as "the most potential part of rhetoric", and he even claims that the name of rhetoric, *eloquentia*, derives from *elocutio*.[13] Style is then defined as "the suitability of words and sayings for a clear exposition of the arguments discovered and arranged".[14] The quotation indicates that style must be subordinated to the factual content of the speech, its invention and disposition, whereby Vico affirms Aristotle's idea of rhetoric. Moreover, Vico's definition of style, a striking choice of words, indicates that he does not share the idea of style as external ornamentation. In fact, Vico's stance is tricky: on one hand, he demands a lucid and direct language; on the other hand, he insists that such a demand cannot be fulfilled without considerable stylistic sensitivity. Vico underlines this position by referring to Cicero's statement that the speaker must know how to deliver his speech in an elegant manner, but also the subject matter at hand; Cicero believed in a unity of eloquence and wisdom, an idea which Vico supports throughout his authorship.[15] This basic attitude of Vico towards style bears some similarity to the one of Peregrini, who discarded the kind of eloquence which is exclusively occupied with harmonious relations of words, e.g. the *acutezza leggiadria*, and who argued in favour of *acutezza mirabile*, where a semantic content is also present.

From this point of view the notion *sententia*, a saying or proverb, is central to Vico's reflections on rhetoric, because it is an expression in which form and content are chosen extremely suitably. Such sayings were widely used in Roman jurisprudence, where the content, *res*, signifies a common, exterior reality, which is the focus of the juridical debate; and where form, *verbum*, is an apt form of expression. This coincidence of form and content made the notion attractive to the literary mannerism, since it was both amusing, because of its style, and instructing, because of its content.[16] Peregrini too picked up this notion: he distinguished *acutezza leggiadria* from *acutezza mirabile*, claiming that only the last kind of *acutezza* possesses a harmony between the words which is affirmed on a semantic level; therefore, he identifies *sententia* with *acutezze seriose*, i.e. *acutezze mirabili.*[17]

For the same reason Vico uses the notion *sententia*, which he treats at length in his *Institutiones oratoriae*, § 35, entitled *De sententiis, vulgo 'del ben parlare in concetti' (On Sayings, Commonly Called 'to Speak in Aphorisms')*. Here Vico identifies the Latin notion *sententia* with the Aristotelian notion *gnome*, described in Aristotle's *Rhetoric,*[18] claiming that the use of a *gnome* recurs in the Italian literary mannerism, called by Vico "il concettismo", and in which Peregrini is a prominent figure.[19] As in Peregrini's *Delle acutezze*, we also find considerations in Vico's *Institutiones oratoriae* on the epistemological capacity to create stylistic expressions with a semantic content, namely reflections on ingenuity.

2. Ingenuity

As we have seen, Vico conceives of rhetoric as a theory of argumentation, and by style he understands an expression which aptly describes the subject matter. His idea of ingenuity is developed within this framework: ingenuity is the ability to produce statements where form and content are united in a striking manner. Vico takes over the idea of ingenuity from Peregrini: "The power of ingenuity, as Matteo Peregrini has said in his golden book *Delle acutezze*, consists in mutually relating different things."[20] Accordingly, Peregrini's notion *acutezza mirabile*, which involves ingenuity, is valuable to Vico. A special variant of *acutezza mirabile* is, as I have already explained, an embellished enthymeme, which is also called an acute saying, *detto acuto*. Vico also takes over this notion of *detto acuto* from Peregrini.[21]

Vico states of the enthymematic inference containing such an embellishment, that an "enthymematic force" is needed.[22] He explains that this force is a certain acuteness, *acumen*, with the ability to relate ideas through the form of expression, and he goes on, stating that "Peregrini defines acuteness, the power of ingenuity, as 'the happy invention of a means which connects different things in one sentence with a wondrous aptness and through a high degree of elegance'".[23] Vico mentions Aristotle as the ultimate source for this definition of ingenuity, able to connect separate ideas through rhetorical figures, and among those the metaphor as the foremost. Thus Vico quotes from Aristotle's *Rhetoric,* that "only the clever and acute philosophers are able to recognise similarity between distant things",[24] and from his *Poetics,* that "to use metaphor is especially difficult, and only possible for the versatile mind".[25] Vico adds that this ability to discover likeness between different things is also crucial in relation to *dicta acuta.*

So far, it seems as if Vico is in agreement with Peregrini regarding his idea about ingenuity. Nevertheless, Vico disagrees with Peregrini on the question of the cognitive status of the operation of ingenuity. In relation to *detti acuti,* Peregrini had made a sharp distinction between intellect and ingenuity: the latter is assigned a hedonistic and non–cognitive role, to please the listeners through its invention of embellishment of the enthymeme; the former, on the other hand, is assigned a pedagogical and cognitive role, to present the subject matter of the enthymeme in a truthful manner.[26] Vico agrees with Peregrini on one point, namely that the work of ingenuity is the artifice, but, as we shall see, he refuses to accept the non–cognitive role assigned to this faculty by Peregrini.[27] Vico draws attention to another of the mannerists, Sforza Pallavicino, "the most acute thinker".[28] Pallavicino had published *Trattato dello stilo e del dialogo* in 1662, twenty-three years after Peregrini's *Delle acutezze,* and after years of friendship with Peregrini.[29] In this book, Pallavicino criticises Peregrini's distinction between intellect and ingenuity:

> Even though the intellect is pleased by the simple contemplation of beauty, as I described in another book, its more noble and more satisfying faculty of judgement will not be fascinated unless the object contemplated contains some truth.[30]

Vico may refer to this passage in *Institutiones oratoriae,* claiming that according to Pallavicino *dicta acuta* give rise to wonder, which again gives way for a flash of insight. In fact, Vico says, this particular satisfaction of the intellect is the real cause of pleasure of the *dicta acuta.*[31] This remarkable analysis of aesthetic fascination means that the role of ingenuity, to create the expression of *dicta acuta,* cannot be reduced to a pure aesthetic one; the role of ingenuity has, in the end, a cognitive role too; only that beauty will fascinate which seems to reveal some unknown truth. Vico concludes that *dictum acutum* is the font and origin of knowledge; the highest pleasure possible to the intellect.[32] That is a significant statement. Tesauro and Peregrini had conceived of science or truth as a field of philosophy; and eloquence, or beauty, as the field of rhetoric. Vico rejects this dichotomy, claiming that language and knowledge are inseparable, and that the wonder caused by literary style may well lead to knowledge.[33] Having reached this point, Vico turns against Peregrini and his dichotomy between intellect and ingenuity: "When hearing an acute remark, nothing prevents the intellect to be easily and briefly instructed and ingenuity pleased by its beauty at the same time."[34]

But even this description of the role of ingenuity is too humble according to Vico. Truly, ingenuity may be pleased by beauty and the intellect may be instructed at the same time; but the association of different ideas, which takes place through the artifice in acute remarks, is made possible through the stylistic operation of ingenuity; it is exactly this aesthetic enterprise that provides the new and unknown order of ideas which in turn are recognised by the intellect. Therefore, Vico triumphs: "but the origin to all acute remarks is this: truth, which is hidden but clearly and easily revealed through a new and rare invention."[35] From the context it is clear that by "invention" he means creation of artifice. This statement is more radical than the above–mentioned claim of a parallelism between intellect and ingenuity, since Vico here assigns epistemological consequences to the stylistic sensibility and creativity of ingenuity; the invention of forms of acute remarks is regarded as a medium for creating new perspectives, through which relations between ideas, truth, can be recognised by the intellect. In other words, Vico regards ingenuity as a cognitive faculty.

This point of view is quite another from the one we have seen advanced by Peregrini, where the non–cognitive and aesthetic pleasure of ingenuity is nothing but parallel to the recognition of the intellect. Still, as I have pointed out, the consequence which Vico draws from Peregrini's concept of ingenuity, was implicit in Peregrini's notion of *acutezza mirabile*. But it seems as if Peregrini, though critical towards the contemporary cult of stylistic pomp of ingenuity, were not able to free himself from the conception of ingenuity as a non–cognitive faculty. But Vico, even though he basically regards rhetoric as a theory of argumentation, regards style as the most powerful part of rhetoric.

Vico's remarks on the entangled relationship between language and knowledge, and likewise his idea of ingenuity, are quite original in the tradition of rhetoric. According to Cicero, the task of ingenuity is to invent or discover the middle term of a syllogistic argument; the art of topics is a vehicle to discover material for this syllogism, or eventually the enthymeme. Cicero is not specific about the nature of this invention, but it seems as if it is regarded as a logical operation.[36] In the Italian literary mannerism we see a changed conception of rhetoric, now regarded as a theory of ornamentation and not one of argumentation. In consequence, the inventions characteristic to ingenuity do not regard the subject matter, but refined rhetorical figures. Vico's contribution to the tradition of rhetoric is double: Firstly, he rejects the idea of rhetoric as a pure theory of ornamentation, thus affirming the classical idea of rhetoric. Secondly, he elaborates and incorporates Peregrini's and Pallavicino's theory of the cognitive power of stylistic sensibility and creativity. This allows him to formulate a new concept of ingenuity, where the invention of the argument's middle term is unfolded through the artifice; the invention or discovery of subject matters and their true relation does not happened within a logical reasoning, but within an aesthetic one.[37]

3. Vico's Defence against Neo–classicism

All these memorable reflections on acute remarks were stated in Vico's *Institutiones oratoriae*, in the section named *De sententiis, vulgo 'del ben parlare in concetti'*, dictated during the academic year 1710–1711. It turns out that they were advanced as a response to actual criticism. Vico notes that an anonymous Italian, in a book named *L'arte di ben pensare* (The Art of Reasoning), had quoted another anonymous writer, a Frenchman, for claiming that all acute remarks are reducible to "falseness appearing as truth", or "truth appearing as falseness"; acute remarks are stylish, but somewhat deceptive statements.[38]

Sorrentino has identified the anonymous Frenchman with Domenico Bouhours, whose book, *La maniere de bien penser dans les ouvrages d'esprit*, was published in Lyon in 1691; and the anonymous Italian with Giuseppe Orsi (1652–1733), who had written *Considerazioni sopra un famoso libro francese intitolato: 'La maniera di ben pensare'* (Cosiderations about a Famous French Book Entitled 'The Art of Reasoning'), published in Bologna in 1703. According to Sorrentino, Orsi introduced Bouhours' claim that truth is a loyal representation of reality, which means that *acutezza* is nothing but falseness; acute remarks are never true in their literal sense, only if they are understood in a subtle analogical sense, and that understanding depends upon the ability to grasp the metaphorical arguments suggested through the artifice. Orsi's book was followed by a long discussion among the Italians about the dignity, or lack of dignity, of Italian art and literature, since *acutezza* was such an important element in it. This discussion continued until 1710, and Vico's section, *De sententiis, vulgo 'del ben parlare in concetti'*, may be understood as a contribute to this debate.[39]

Vico defends the nobility of mannerists' theory of acute remarks through examples demonstrating their inherent, logical validity, and he adds polemically that anyone capable of creating acute remarks must possess a sane judgement, *ars iudicandi*. This is a provocative remark, since the neo–classicists had criticised literati of mannerist literature and rhetoric for being unable to control their deceptive, overrefined and feeble manner of speaking.[40] On the other hand, Vico does not reject the existence of remarks deserving Bouhour's description, falseness appearing as truth, but according to Vico, these remarks are not the acute ones, *dicta acuta*, but *dicta arguta*: "acuta enim docent, arguta fallunt" (acute remarks instruct; witty remarks deceive).[41] This distinction goes back to Cicero, who claimed in *De optimo genere oratorum* that "in order to teach the speaker should use acute (*acuta*) remarks; in order to amuse he should use witty (*arguta*) remarks; and in order to move he should use serious (*graves*) ones".[42] According to Vico, it is only the kind of remarks called *arguta*, and not *acuta*, which deserve the description of Bouhours, "falseness appearing as truth". The Latin dichotomy *dictum acutum* versus *dictum argutum* corresponds to a dichotomy in Italian; *acutezza* corresponds to *dictum acutum*; and *argutezza*, or *arguzie*, corresponds to *dictum argutum*. Vico's defence of

Italian mannerism against French neo–classicism is based on this distinction.

Vico explains that *dictum argutum* is identical with Aristotle's "apparent enthymeme", in which the true cause is replaced with something else which is not the cause. Only in this instance, Vico says, may we speak of "falseness" as Bouhours did. This kind of falseness, however, is easy to detect, because *dictum argutum*, which is a wordplay based entirely on the harmony between the words, is totally spoiled if one single word is replaced by a synonym; but *dictum acutum* remains intact after such a replacement, since this kind of remark is based on the semantic structure of the sentence. Therefore Vico agrees with Aristotle and Cicero on the disgracefulness of *dictum argutum*, because of the deception, but he underlines their harmlessness, arguing that man avoids falseness by instinct.[43]

Although the distinction between acute and witty remarks is mentioned by Cicero, it is very probable that Vico knew it from Emanuele Tesauro, who plays upon it, and to whom *argutezza* is a key–concept in his *Il cannocchiale aristotelico,* dating from 1654. Tesauro thus claims about *argutezza,* a witty saying:

> Now, having reflected upon these witty sayings and discussing this matter theoretically, I shall say that perfect wits and ingenious concepts are nothing but urbanely fallacious arguments. And principally you will agree with me that not every argument is witty, though ingenious. Because, if you quote that famous theorem of Euclid for me, that "in a triangle all three sides are equal because all the lines which are drawn directly from the centre to the circumference are equal", then I shall say that this is a truly ingenious piece of mathematical speculation, but not a witty one. And similarly, if I asked you for what reason the hail falls during the summer and not during the winter, should you reply to me that the second region[44] of air in winter is warm, and cold during the summer because of the antiperistasis,[45] and that therefore the vapour which is there freezes during the summer and not during the winter, this would by all means be a truly beautiful and learned meteorological answer; but you would not place it among those witty answers, nor would you call it an epigrammatic concept, even if you dressed it in a poetic metre,

since the reason is in itself true and conclusive, even without any invention of the intellect. It is therefore necessary that a witty argument gains its force through ingenuity, that is, through some subtle invention, so that it truely may be called one of our concepts. It is for this reason that Macrobius, using the Greek term, called witty remarks *scommata*,[46] that is, jests; and in his *Ethics*[47] our author, when talking about the urban man and ingenuity, quick to deliver witty remarks, called him *euscoptonta*,[48] that is, "a good jester",[49] and Seneca defined *argutezze* as "clever and subtle conclusions",[50] that is, paralogisms,[51] corresponding exactly to the final words of epigrams. And in order that you may realise that this is true, recall the examination of those ten *argutezze* which I have presented for you as examples. Each of them, unfolded in verses, would form a witty epigram, and you will find that they are all based upon one or another of the fallacious *topoi*, which our author called "*topoi* of apparent enthymemes".[52] The reason is that these enthymemes surprise the intellect, first appearing effective, but once examined attentively they dissolve into empty fallacies...Therefore I shall conclude by saying that the only praise for *argutezze* consists in knowing how to lie well.[53]

Tesauro may not be as cynical as he appears to be, since even "false" enthymemes are conceived as a "veil" through which reality can be recognised.[54] These fictions are very useful in informal communication, and Tesauro regards them as important in rhetoric. Accordingly, he sees a chasm between rhetoric and logic: the speaker must be able to create such fictitious *argutezze*, while it is not necessary to the logician, to whom it is sufficient to know the rules of logic and follow them in his search for truth.[55] Just like Peregrini, Tesauro conceives of the *argutezze* of the speaker as autonomous in relation to reality; the only difference is that Tesauro characterises the sayings of the speaker as direct falsehoods, while Peregrini defines them as beautiful—still in opposition to truth. Compared to Peregrini and Tesauro, Vico takes an original stance, since he denies the radical distinction between rhetoric and philosophy, that is, between form of expression and knowledge.

Vico thus replies to Bouhours by condemning *dicta arguta*, the false enthymemes advocated by Tesauro, and by defending *dicta acuta*, emblematic to Peregrini. In Vico's autobiography we do find a parallel to this position, when he relates his own occupation with poetry while young. Here he claims that as a youngster he was "cutting off the depraved part of modern poetry, which is nothing but amusing falseness".[56] He also states about the poetry which he wrote as young that "Vico regarded this kind of art as nothing but an exercise of ingenuity in creating *argutezza*, which is pleasing for its falseness".[57] In fact, this distinction between *argutezza* and *acutezza* is clear already on the first page of his autobiography, where he writes that he grew up with a "melancholic and sharp nature, which is said to be characteristic of ingenious and profound men, whose ingenuity flashes with *acutezze*, and who do not find pleasure in *arguzie* or falsity".[58] The distinction between *argutus* and *acutus* was obviously fundamental to Vico, also on a personal level; *dictum argutum* could be subjected to the criticism of neo–classicism for its falsity; but *dictum acutum* could not, wherefore Vico defends this notion from the Italian literary mannerism. If it is true that Vico had Tesauro in mind when referring to the notion *argutezza*, it is still an open question whether the daring Tesauro, maybe too daring to Arcadia, had any influence on the young Vico. I shall return to this question below.

Having pointed out *dictum argutum* as the proper object of Bouhours' criticism, Vico elaborates the notion of *dictum acutum*. He refers to Cicero who, contrary to Bouhours, regards acute remarks as a way of expressing an original conception.[59] In relation to this, Cicero claims that eloquence is composed of two disciplines; one concerned with the invention or discovery of arguments useful for the speech, *ars inveniendi*; and another one explaining how to arrange these arguments in a logically valid way, *ars iudicandi*.[60] Furthermore, in *Topica* Cicero lists all the pigeon-holes, *loci*, which the speaker can check in order to discover his arguments. Vico, however, does not refer to *Topica*, but to Cicero's comment in *De oratore*, that a list of *loci*, as the one provided in *Topica*, is insufficient to discover arguments; only the sharp mind, *acer ingenium*, of the searching speaker is able to discover those arguments.[61] Therefore, Vico claims that according to Cicero, the source of acute remarks is ingenuity itself.

Peregrini may be a possible inspiration for Vico's point of view. In *I fonti dell'ingegno ridotti ad arte*, Peregrini notes that topics is not any longer regarded as a useful checklist for the speaker who wants to discover new arguments, but simply as an insignificant branch of rhetoric. He does not, however, deplore this state of topics, but points out a better means for the discovery in question: ingenuity, the ability to experience an abundance of relations from a hint. This capacity should be regarded as a much better substitute to the traditional art of topics.[62] Vico, however, did not make any explicit reference to this work, and we cannot know whether or not he knew it.

The conception of the art of topics, as intimately bound to ingenuity, is indicated by Vico several places in *Institutiones oratoriae*. In § 9, *De inventione*, and in § 11, *De arte topica*, he lists all the *loci* which traditionally belong to topics. But immediately after, in § 12, *Exempla locorum*, he claims that it is not a proper task for a schoolbook in rhetoric to provide rules for the art of topics, because every single *locus* must be found within the concrete situation.[63] The art of topics should not be regarded as a formal list mechanically providing the *loci*; instead, the art of topics should be understood as an art guiding the ability to investigate every single situation with discernment. Is Vico thus giving up the traditional idea of topics, in order to redefine it from an epistemological point of view, as an empirical logic? This presumption is confirmed in *De sapientia antiquissima italorum* (On the Wisdom of the Ancient Italians), published in 1710, and in the polemic following in the two subsequent years. Here we see Vico defend his highly original conception of topics as an art guiding the faculty of apprehension, *facultas percipiendi*.[64] I shall deal with this idea of topics, but before doing so I shall first outline Vico's theory of knowledge, in which this *facultas percipiendi* must be understood; then I shall outline Descartes' reflections regarding the art of topics, and then, in the last chapter, I shall focus on Vico's original idea of topics.

Notes

1   Vico, *Vita, Opere* V, pp. 8f.
2   See Toffanin, *L'Arcadia*, pp. 6f, 24.
3   Battistini's note in Vico, *Opere,* ed. Battistini, p. xl.
4   Vico, *Institutiones oratoriae, Opere* VIII, § 1, p. 159: "Rhetorica sive eloquentia est facultas dicendi apposite ad persuadendum."
5   Aristotle, *Rhetoric* 11354a–1356a.
6   See Cicero, *De optimo genere oratorum* 1.3; Quintilian, *Institutio oratoria* 12.10.
7   Vico, *Institutiones oratoriae, Opere* VIII, p. 160, § 2.
8   *Ibid.*, p. 160, § 3.
9   Aristotle, *Nicomachean Ethics* 1140a–1141a; *ibid., Rhetoric* 1354a, 1355a.
10   *Ibid., Rhetoric* 1358b.
11   Vico, *Institutiones oratoriae, Opere* VIII, § 3, p. 160. These three fields are treated in §§ 18, 19 and 20.
12   *Ibid.*, § 8, p. 162. Vico thus treats *inventio* in §§ 9–21; *dispositio* in §§ 22–31, *elocutio* in §§32–52; and *memoria et pronuntiatio* in § 53. Compare Cicero, *De oratore* 1.31.142.
13   Vico, *Institutiones oratoriae, Opere* VIII, § 32, p. 170.
14   *Ibid.*: "Idoneorum verborum et sententiarum ad res inventas et dispositas accommodata expositio."
15   Cicero, *De inventione* 1.1.1. Vico, *Institutiones oratoriae, Opere* VIII, § 7, p. 162; *De ratione, Opere* I, pp. 81ff. This point of view is also defended in Vico's speech of 1737, *Le accademie e i rapporti tra la filosofia e l'eloquenza, Opere* VII, p. 36: "...l'eloquenza non è altro che la sapienza che parla." And in *Scienza nuova seconda*: philosophy deals with the apodictic true, "il vero", while philology treats the certain, "il certo". See *Scienza nuova seconda, Opere* IV, §§ 137–141.
16   Mooney, *Vico in the Tradition of Rhetoric*, p. 142.
17   Peregrini, *Delle acutezze*, pp. 135–137.
18   Aristotle, *Rhetoric* 1394.
19   Vico, *Institutiones oratoriae, Opere* VIII, § 35, pp. 182–184.
20   *Ibid.*, p. 183: "Ingenii virtus, ut Matthaeus Peregrinius in aureo 'De acutis dictis' libello disserit, consistit in mutuo diversarum rerum ligamine."
21   *Ibid.*, p. 183.
22   *Ibid.*: "Vis enthymemiatica." See Peregrini, *Delle acutezze*, p. 122.
23   Vico, *Institutiones oratoriae, Opere* VIII, § 35, p. 183: "Hinc idem Peregrinius acumen seu ingenii vim definit 'felicem medii inventionem, quod in dicto aliquo diversas res mira aptitudine et per summam elegantiam colligat.'" See Peregrini, *Delle acutezze*, p. 120.
24   Vico, *Institutiones oratoriae, Opere* VIII, § 35, p. 184: "Soli philosophi solertes acutique praestare possunt in rebus distantibus quid simile contemplari." The quotation may derive from Aristotle's *Rhetoric* 1412a.
25   Vico, *Institutiones oratoriae, Opere* VIII, § 35, pp. 183f: "Decenter uti translationibus maxime est arduum, nam nonnisi versatilis ingenii est." This idea may be inspired from Aristotle's *Poetics* 1459a.
26   Peregrini, *Delle acutezze*, pp. 122f.
27   Vico, *Institutiones oratoriae, Opere* VIII, § 35, p. 184: "Sed nihil magis, nam acumen non constituitur a materia et obiecti novitate, sed ab artificio." Quoted

from Peregrini, *Delle acutzze*, p. 122: "In somma, l'artificio ha luogo solamente o principalmente non già nel trovar cose belle, ma nel farle." And Vico affirms Peregrini's dichotomy between ingenuity and intellect: Vico, *Institutiones oratoriae, Opere* VIII, § 35, p. 185: "Verum autem intellectus obiectum est, pulchrum autem ingenii." This conception can be found in Peregrini, *Delle acutezze*, p. 122.

28 Vico, *Institutiones oratoriae, Opere* VIII, § 35, pp. 184f.

29 *Trattatisti e narratori del seicento*, editor's preface to Pallavicino's *Trattato dello stile e del dialogo*, p. 194.

30 Pallavicino, *Trattato dello stile e del dialogo*, p. 198: "L'intelletto in somma, benché secondo la semplice operazione dell'apprendere si compiaccia nella contemplazione del bello, come in altro libro io mostrai, tuttavia secondo quella più nobile e più dilettosa del giudicare non ha vaghezza se non del vero."

31 Vico, *Institutiones oratoriae, Opere* VIII, § 35, pp. 184f.

32 *Ibid.* p. 185: "Quae scientiae acquisitio fons est et origo summae voluptatis, qua intellectus humanus affici possit."

33 See Cesare, "Sul concetto di metafora in Giambattista Vico," p. 215.

34 Vico, *Institutiones oratoriae, Opere* VIII, § 35, p. 185: "Sed nihil vetat quin, acuto dicto audito, et intelletus brevi et facile doceatur, et pulchro ingenium delectetur."

35 *Ibid.*, p. 187: "Sed omnium unam esse originem: verum quod lateat ac novo raroque invento medio celeriter et facile detegatur."

36 Cicero, *Topica* 1.2.6–8; *De oratore* 2.39.162–2.41.175, in particular 174.

37 See Vico, *Institutiones oratoriae, Opere* VIII, § 35, pp. 185, 187.

38 *Ibid.*, p. 186. See Mooney, *Vico in the Tradition of Rhetoric*, p. 156.

39 Sorrentino, *La retorica e la poetica di Vico. Ossia la prima concezione estetica del linguaggio*, pp. 85–89.

40 Vico, *Institutiones oratoriae, Opere* VIII, § 35, pp. 187f.

41 *Ibid.*, p. 188.

42 Cicero, *De optimo genere oratorum* 1.5: "Sunt enim docendi acutae, delectandi quasi argutae, commovendi graves."

43 Vico, *Institutiones oratoriae, Opere* VIII, § 35, pp. 188f.

44 "Seconda region": see Seneca, *Naturales quaestiones* 4.3.1f.

45 "Antiperistasis": opposition of pressures.

46 "Scommata": jests. See Macrobius, *Saturnalia* 7.3.2.

47 Aristotle, *Nichomachean Ethics* 1128a.

48 "Euscoptonta": keen–sighted.

49 "Bonum cavillatorem."

50 "Conclusiunculae vafrae et callidae."

51 A piece of false reasoning.

52 "Apperentium enthumematum loci." See Aristotle, *Rhetoric* 1400b.

53 Tesauro, *Il cannocchiale aristotelico*, pp. 94f: "Or sopra questi arguti detti riflettendo, e sopra tutta questa materia teoricamente dalla sua fonte discorrendo, io dico, le perfette argutezze e gli 'ingegnosi concetti non esser altro che argomenti urbanamente fallaci. E principalmente ben mi consentirai tu non ogni argomento, benché ingegnoso, essere arguto. Però che, se tu mi reciti quell'argomento di Euclide, che il 'il triangolo ha gli tre lati eguali però che tutte le linee dirittamente tirate dal centro alla circonferenza sono eguali fra loro,' ell'è veramente una ingegnosa specolazion matematica, ma non è arguta. E similmente, ricercandoti io per qual cagione la gragnuola cada la state e non il verno, se tu mi rispondi che la seconda region dell'aria d'inverno è calda, di estate è fredda per l'antiperistsi, e

perciò il vapor colà pervenuto di state si congela e non d'inverno, l'è bella veramente e dotta risposta meterologica, ma non tu l'annoveraresti fra quelle risposte argute, né tu la chiamerresti concetto di epigramma, benché tu la travesti di poetico metro, però che la ragione per se medesima senz'alcun fingimento dell'intelletto è cosa vera e concludente. Egli è dunque necessario che l'argomento arguto abbia sua forza per forz d'ingegno, cioè per alcun fingimento cavilloso, onde veramente si chiami concetto nostro. Che perciò i motti arguti da Macrobio grecamente son detti *scommata*, cioè cavillazioni; e il nostro autore nella divina sua *Etica*, discorrendo dell'uomo urbano e d'ingegno pronto a' motti arguti, chiamollo *euscoptonta*, cioè 'bonum cavillatorem'; e Seneca diffinì le argutezze 'conclusiunculae vafrae et callidae', cioè paralogismi, corrispondenti apunto alle chiuse degli epigrammi. E che questo sia il vero, richiama alla esamina quelle diece argutezze che ti ho proposte per idea; ciascuna delle quali, spiegata inversi, formerebbe un epigramma arguto: e tutte le troverai fondate in alcun de' topici fallaci, che dall'autor nostro s'intitolarono *apparentium enthymematum loci*. Però che ad udirle sorprendono l'intelletto, parendo concludenti di primo incontro, ma esaminate si risolvono in una vana fallacia."; *ibid*, p. 97: "Talché io conchiudo l'unica loda delle argutezze consistere nel sapere ben mentire."

54   *Ibid.*, pp. 75, 88.
55   *Ibid.*, pp. 98f.
56   Vico, *Vita, Opere* V, p. 8: "...spampinava nelle maniere piú corotte del poetare moderno che con altro non diletta che coi trascorsi e col falso."
57   *Ibid*, p. 9: "Ma il Vico aveva appresa una tal sorta di poesia per un esercizio d'ingegno in opere d'argutezza, la quale unicamente diletta col falso..."
58   *Ibid.*, p. 1: "...di una natura malinconica ed acre, qual dee essere degli uomini ingegnosi e profondi che per l'ingegno balenino in acutezze, per la riflessione non si dilettino dell'arguzie e del falso." Vico repeats this conception in his answer to the German review *Acta eruditorum*, wherein Vico's *Scienza nuova prima* was called "more ingenious than true." See Vico, *Vici vindiciae, Opere* III, pp. 304f.
59   *Ibid.*, *Institutiones oratoriae, Opere* VIII, § 35, p. 186.
60   Cicero, *Topica* 2.6–8.
61   *Ibid.*, *De oratore* 2.162–175, especially 162 and 174.
62   Peregrini, *I fonti dell'ingegno ridotti ad arte*, pp. 175, 180. See Battistini & Raimondi, *Le figure della retorica*, p. 172; Lange, *Theoretiker des literarischen Manierismus*, p. 141.
63   The central sentence, "tradere praecepta nostrae provinciae non est", is appearently cut out in Gentile and Nicolini's edition of *Institutiones oratoriae*, wherefore I quote Crifò's: § 14, *Exempla locorum*, p. 54. See Giuliani, "Vicos Rhetorical Philosophy and the New Rhetoric", p. 34.
64   Vico, *De sapientia, Opere* I, p. 180.

Chapter Three

Vico's Theory of Knowledge

1. Faculties of Cognition

Inspired by etymologies of Etruscan origin, Vico puts forward an epistemology comprising five basic faculties: sensation, fantasy, memory, intellect and ingenuity.[1] According to Vico, sensation is the source of knowledge. He refers to the Aristotelian principle: "the human mind perceives everything through the senses, as the Aristotelians have it."[2] This empirical position remains unchanged throughout the rest of Vico's writings—it is even traceable in *Scienza nuova seconda*, dating from the year of his death, 1744: "there is nothing in the intellect, which is not derived from sensation."[3]

Aristotle had formulated this principle in *On the Soul*,[4] but at the time of Vico it was widely diffused, and had also found its advocate in the French philosopher Pierre Gassendi (1592–1655), who had made references to this statement in his major work *Syntagma philosophicum* (Philosophical Compendium, 1649).[5] Vico recalls in his autobiography how Gassendi's introduction of the Greek philosopher Epicurus (341–271 BC), via the Latin poet and philosopher Lucretius (98–55 BC) and his work *On Nature*, had an enormous influence in Naples in the period just before Vico left the city in order to teach at Vatolla.[6] Furthermore, Vico seems to have been inspired by this movement. In the first place, he picked up Gassendi's nominalism, negating the chasm which Descartes had made between sensation and reason. In the second place, Vico was influenced by Gassendi's probabilism, by which Gassendi holds that although human cognition of nature has no absolute certainty—as Descartes insisted—it is not impossible; we can make use of our empirical observations in order to establish hypotheses about nature.[7]

How did Vico elaborate these general principles into a theory of knowledge? In the first place, Vico did not conceive of sensation as a passive reception of sense impressions, but on the contrary, as an active creation; sense impressions must be ordered into a form by the perceiving subject, if they are to be experienced as real. Vico argues as follows: "For if the senses are faculties, then we make things have colour by seeing them, things have taste by tasting them, things have coldness or heat by touching them."[8]

Fantasy must be understood in close association with sensation, because fantasy forms the single sense impressions into a coherent whole, which is experienced as concrete and certain. This concreteness has a visual character in the mind of the perceiving subject. It is the work of fantasy to create these mental images (*imagines*).[9] Apart from making mental images from sense impressions, fantasy also associates these mental images with emotions.[10] Emotions may, however, themselves evoke reflections on experience, as is characteristic of the manner in which poets reflect.[11]

The fact that fantasy and sense impressions are interrelated in this intimate way, makes Vico identify fantasy and memory: memory creates images from previous sense impressions, just as fantasy creates images from actual perception.[12] Consequently, to imagine is simply to memorise previous sensations; according to Vico, the human mind cannot imagine anything which is not a reminiscence of an earlier sensation or a combination of sensations.[13] This identification means that memory—as well as images created by fantasy—is inseparably bound up with emotions.

Apart from sensation, fantasy and memory, Vico adds yet another notion to his theory of knowledge, namely *sensus communis* which is a common, moral feeling in a social community. He then relates *sensus communis* with *prudentia*, prudence or practical wisdom, which is the moral and social idea about the proper action in a specific situation in a particular community. These epistemological concepts—*sensus communis* and *prudentia*—are important in Vico's defence of social sciences and rhetoric.[14] Aristotle made this association possible by placing the Greek word *phronesis*, corresponding to the Latin *prudentia*, in the core of his reflections on social sciences and rhetoric.[15]

Sensation, fantasy, memory and *sensus communis* are interrelated and concern empirical reality. The intellect, on the other hand, is a formal faculty. It is directed against a man–made and fictitious world, as opposed to the first four faculties, which are directed against the created and given world.[16] For example mathematics is a man–made discipline, and it is subjected to the examination of the intellect. Ingenuity is a rational faculty like the intellect but, contrary to the intellect, it is related to the faculties directed towards the empirical world.

When Vico defines ingenuity in *De sapientia* from an epistemological point of view, he applies the linguistic approach well–known from his *Institutiones oratoriae*: "'Ingenuity' means the faculty of connecting different things in one sentence."[17] Rather remarkably, Vico claims that the material for this task of connecting is not words, but mental images, previously formed of sense impressions by fantasy and memory. For this reason Vico calls fantasy "the eye of ingenuity".[18] Fantasy is thus inserted between sensation and ingenuity. Consequently, the acuteness and swiftness of ingenuity is vital to the flexibility and precision of sensation and memory. It is not the sensibility of the sense organs which, in itself, provides the human mind with a pregnant impression; on the contrary, the sensibility and flexibility with which ingenuity searches sense impressions, transmitted by sensation, is decisive for the quality of sensation; as Mooney puts it, "the sharper our ingenuity, the keener is our perception, the more certain our knowledge".[19]

In order to explain ingenuity, Vico presents an etymology of the Latin wherein ingenuity, *ingenium,* is identified with nature, *natura*: *natura* is derived from *nascor,* to be born; *ingenium* is derived from *gigno,* to create or produce. Therefore, nature and ingenuity are analogical, since they both possess a creative power.[20] He repeats this etymology in his autobiography, adding, in agreement with his *Institutiones oratoriae*, that the most important feature of ingenuity is its *acutezza*.[21] What is the philosophical reason for the identification between *ingenium* and *natura*? Vico argues that this etymology can be explained in one of two ways: either the Latins thought it essential to ingenuity to be able to recognise what is "suitable, becoming, noble or base" in a given situation;[22] or, because the Latins conceived of man as a creator in the field of crafts, in a similar way to God, who is the creator of this world: "As God is the creator of nature, man is the creator of crafts."[23]

The first explanation might be understood as an epistemological counterpart to the linguistic ability of ingenuity to express diverse ideas in one sentence: on a epistemological level the "suitable" means the discovery of relevant ideas or experiences, and their true relation; on a linguistic level, the "suitable" refers to the role of style, in creating a harmonic relation between the words which, of course, must express the content aptly. This conception of ingenuity as stated in *De sapientia,* can also be found in Vico's *Institutiones oratoriae*:

> It must be sharp and quick–witted, able to go immediately to the heart of the issue at hand, seeing every facet there is to see about it and bringing them all together into a fruitful unity; it must be simple in expression, able to make the meaning in the thoughts and the thoughts in the words clearer than glass; and it must be versatile, swifter than Proteus in moving from light to serious matters, from gentle to harsh, from simple ones to challenging ones, and from a style that is grand to one that is moderate, then plain.[24]

According to Vico, the "suitable" marks a capacity to grasp and express a historically situated problem, and to find a solution apt for the context. To Plato, this is insufficient for a speaker intending to guide a social group: the speaker must possess knowledge of transcendent proportions according to which everyone must live. Plato thus holds that the "suitable" in a given situation should be deduced from a transcendent, non–historical and static sphere.[25] Vico, on the other hand, claims that such a judgement should arise from knowledge about an empirical and social world in its organic wholeness.

To turn to the second explanation: what did Vico mean by describing man as a creator of crafts, arts and science, in a similar way to God, who is the creator of nature? Vico explains that man's creativity in all these disciplines should be regarded as the result of a basic capacity to order some given thing into beautiful proportions. According to the Etruscans, what is well understood, *scitum*, will appear as well ordered, *pulchrum*, to the percipient, and therefore *scitum* is synonymous with *pulchrum*.[26] The synonymity suggests that experience, basic to science and the other disciplines mentioned above, is guided by the faculty of ingenuity, and, most importantly, that this faculty works through an aesthetic sensibility. This general characteristic of ingenuity, advanced in *De sapientia*, is not in conflict with the definition in *Institutiones oratoriae*, where ingenuity is defined as the ability to relate several ideas through their expression, but it is broader, since it is not confined to the ordering of linguistic material into beautiful and pointed expressions; it deals with a much wider range of mental ordering, fundamental to the arts and sciences.

In turn, neither perception nor knowledge is a passive reception of data, but an active creation. Furthermore, ingenuity, the faculty which allows man to be such a creator, is described by the principle *verum et factum convertuntur* (The true and the made are interchangeable). What is the meaning of this principle?

2. The Principle 'verum et factum convertuntur'
This principle is widely known as Vico adapted it to his philosophy of history, *Scienza nuova*: since mankind has created its own history, it is possible to find the principles of this history within the modifications of

its own mind.[27] Nature, on the other hand, is created by God and therefore not comprehensible to man in the same direct way as history is. The principle itself, *verum et factum convertuntur*, has been interpreted by many scholars and especially in relation to *Scienza nuova*. Among others, we find the idealistic interpretation of Benedetto Croce and that of Wilhelm Dilthey (1833–1911), who saw the principle as a foreshadowing of his own distinction between the humanities and the natural sciences.[28] Far less attention has been given to the principle in the early writings of Vico, although there is good reason for doing so.

Vico offers his earliest explanation of the principle in the section *De vero et facto* (Concerning the True and the Made) in *De sapientia*. Here we find the principle explained by a distinction, inherited from the Latins, between *intelligere*, to apprehend, and *cogitare*, to think: *Intelligere* is regarded as synonymous with *perfecte legere*, to collect, and *aperte cognoscere*, to know clearly; *cogitare,* on the other hand, is synonymous with "pensare", to think, and "andar racogliendo", to collect.[29] In both of the etymologies, true or not, Vico intends to explain knowledge, apprehension or reasoning, as an active "collecting" in relation to the object. Understood in this way, the true and the made are identical. Vico concludes: "To know is to compose the elements of the things."[30] He elaborates this point, saying that this "collecting" should be conceived as an "internal collecting", that is, as a mental, synthesising act.[31] What is "collected" in this mental operation? Vico writes:

> Furthermore, just as words are symbols and signs for ideas, so ideas are symbols and signs for things. Just as reading is the activity of the one who collects the elements of writing [letters] by which the words are made, so knowledge is a collecting of elements of the subject matter, through which the perfect idea about the matter is expressed.[32]

The principle implies an epistemological contrast between God and human beings. God's intellect is unlimited; it contains, disposes and arranges the essence of all existing things and their appearances. The human being, on the other hand, is restricted to knowing things only through their appearances.[33] Consequently, man is forced to accept a phenomenological position and a corresponding nominalism, while God is able to see the essence of things directly and thus allowed an epistemological realism.

What kind of science does this epistemological condition allow human beings? Vico explains that science is also a collecting of "elements" of the objects investigated, that is, a collection of empirical observations from which hypotheses are made. This probabilism, elaborated in *De sapientia,* is also traceable in *De ratione*, where Vico reacts against the tendency of the rationalists to establish mathematics as an ideal for all science. Vico replies: "We are able to prove geometrical truths because we have created geometry; if we were able to prove physical truths, then we would be able to create physical matter."[34] Enough has now been said about the methodological consequences of Vico's principle *verum et factum convertuntur.*

As already stated, fantasy is a central notion in Vico's theory of knowledge.[35] Although it is embedded in an empiricist idea, it makes Vico's theory of knowledge different from empiricist epistemology. Truly, all knowledge must derive from sensation, but Vico underlines the active role of the percipient in the reception of sense impressions; "the given" has to be made "given" to the percipient, by the percipient him— or herself; it cannot be understood as a mere passive reception of sense impression. Here fantasy is important—not as an ability to evoke far fetched ideas, but as an ability to penetrate into reality and its less obvious connections.

The concept of fantasy obviously has an important role in *De sapientia* from 1710. It is, however, also very important in Vico's first inaugural oration from 1699, where we find fantasy described with the same formulations as in *De sapientia* as the ability to create mental images, which represent things; but in this early oration fantasy is also explained in relation to language, especially the use of metaphor.[36] Therefore, one may wonder whether this early speech elucidates Vico's conception of metaphorical reasoning; is it a crossroad between his theory of knowledge and his theory of language? Obviously, stylistic sensibility and creativity is interrelated with achievement of knowledge in this oration.

In 1927, Giovanni Gentile gave an influential philosophical analysis of Vico's first inaugural oration, claiming that it would be unsustainable to identify the notion of fantasy in the oration from 1699 with that in *De sapientia* from 1710, since Vico was influenced by the Neoplatonism of the Renaissance in the years around 1699 and therefore had a completely different idea of fantasy in this first oration.[37] For this reason, I shall examine the interpretation of Gentile, before relating Vico's idea of fantasy, as set forth in his first inaugural oration, to his general theory of knowledge, as it is presented in *De sapientia* from 1710.

3. Vico's First Inaugural Oration of 1699

Gentile identifies two philosophically important periods in Vico's life: one from the publication of *De ratione* in 1708, lasting till the publication of *Risposte* in 1712; the other from 1720, beginning with the publication of *De universi iuris uno principio et fine uno* (On the Principle and Aim of Universal Law), ending with *Scienza nuova seconda* in 1744. By this means Gentile discards any philosophical significance to the time prior to *De ratione*, a period in which Vico's poems and inaugural orations were composed. Gentile argues that Vico, in his autobiography, had expressed satisfaction that these writings had not been published, since, in Vico's view, they did not merit this. Therefore Gentile concludes that Vico had not found his own philosophical stance until 1708.[38]

It is, however, questionable whether Vico's autobiography is a statement about himself as an intellectual, rather than a statement about how Vico would like to be regarded as an intellectual. During these early years in Vico's career, from around 1699 to 1708, and his autobiography from 1725, a profound re–evaluation of mannerism and its literature was taking place among Italian literati, and, as we have seen, even by Vico in his reflections upon the nature of rhetoric, in *Institutiones oratoriae*, dating from 1710–1711. Besides, Vico had participated actively in this movement, but in the 1720s he may certainly have had an interest in playing down his involvement, in order to appear more acceptable to the requirements of the neo–classical movement and to Arcadia. Furthermore, Gentile does not even account for his total silence about the texts which reflect Vico's daily work from 1699 until 1744 as a teacher of rhetoric: *Institutiones oratoriae*.

Gentile's book was published in 1927 and dedicated to his friend Nicolini. Together they edited Vico's *Opere* during the years 1914–1941. It has already been said that Nicolini placed Vico's *Institutiones oratoriae* at the end of the *Opere* in abbreviated form, despite the fact that this text belongs chronologically to the first part of Vico's works. In the first place, it is worth noting that Nicolini reduced the value of Vico's *Institutiones oratoriae* by placing it at the end; secondly, that he discarded passages which refer to central definitions of stylistic notions in the rhetoric of mannerism—a point to which I shall return. In short, Gentile's reading is thus in accord with the interpretation on which Nicolini based his edition of Vico's *Institutiones oratoriae*. In this way, Vico and his relationship to mannerism has been ignored by both of them. As I shall demonstrate below, this allows Gentile to read Vico's first inaugural oration as influenced by the Neoplatonism of the Renaissance. Gentile thus ignores all these men of letters from the seventeenth century who have been presented above as important to the early Vico: Peregrini, Pallavicino and Tesauro. Despite this fact, he quotes Nicolini's biography when he states about the early Vico: "Until 1699 he suffered from the illusion of being more of a poet than a philosopher."[39] If that is so, then why ignore the poetics of the seventeenth century? And why deny that this period might have been philosophically important to Vico?

According to Gentile, Vico's inaugural oration from 1699 is inspired by the idealistic ontology of Plotinus (205–270), but indirectly, through the Neoplatonists of the Renaissance, especially Marsilo Ficino (1433–1499) and Giordano Bruno (1548–1600). The fundamental thought in Neoplatonic ontology is, in brief, that matter is formed by something immaterial and transcendent, called by Plotinus *The One*. Ficino claimed that the communication between matter and *The One* takes place through the Soul of the World, *anima mundi*. This spiritual force controls nature and should be understood as God's continuous emanation in nature. According to Gentile, this idealistic ontology becomes part of Vico's anthropology and philosophy of history through Augustine's idea of grace, which serves as a mediation between the will of God and that of men; God is immanent in nature and in the history of mankind, and his immanence manifests itself in history through providence. When man is seen as an agent within this perspective, Gentile finds it reasonable to talk about man as an *artifex* of history, parallel to God as the *artifex* of nature.[40]

Gentile thus interprets the first inaugural oration as a key–text in his idealistic reading of Vico's authorship. As evidence for this Neoplatonic interpretation, he quotes the following passage:

> Just as God can be known by contemplating the things he has created and which exist in the universe, the human soul may likewise be seen as divine by contemplating its rationality, by which it is outstanding, through its cleverness, its swiftness, its memory and its ingenuity. Certainly, the human soul is an image of God. For just as God is in the world, the soul is in the body. God is infused in the elements of the world, the soul in the parts of the human body. Each acts without involvement of matter, and are without corporeality. And just as God is present everywhere in the world, the soul is present everywhere in the body. Both act independently; separated from any materiality, unmixed with any corporality. God moves the celestial bodies in the ether, hurls lightning in the atmosphere, gives rise to storms on the sea, makes things grow everywhere on earth; but neither the sky or the sea or the earth contain God. The human soul listens with the ear, sees with the eye, becomes angry with the stomach, laughs with the spleen, judges with the heart, understands with the brain, but it has not a specific position in any part of the body. God embraces and rules everything, and outside God nothing exists: the human soul, here using the words of Sallust, is the ruler of mankind, which moves and governs everyone without being ruled itself. God is always active, the human soul is similarly always enterprising. The world exists because God exists; if the world disappeared, God would still exist. The human body perceives because the soul exists; if the body died, the soul would still be immortal.[41]

Gentile calls attention to the apparently idealistic ontology which Vico establishes between the immaterial and the material in this quotation: Between God and nature, and between the human soul and its body. Vico seems to follow Plotinus and the Neoplatonists of the Renaissance insofar as he maintains that something independent and immaterial (God or man's soul) effects something material (matter or the body). Vico adds that "man ascends to God through contemplation".[42] Gentile understands this statement as Vico's complete loyalty to the Neoplatonic tradition, which typically stresses an epistemological movement from external plurality to internal life and from this to something higher, an experience of transcendent unity, or God, what Plotinus calls *The One*.[43]

The decisive step in Gentile's Neoplatonic interpretation is the explanation of 'fantasy' through which God controls man as an *artifex*,[44] and through which he turns man into a creator of all disciplines— science, crafts, arts and religion. Gentile quotes Vico's first oration:

> This faculty, called fantasy, which forms images of things, points out and confirms its divine origin when it creates and brings forth new images: It has invented the minor and the major gods of all peoples, it has invented the heroes. At one moment it changes the images of things, at another it combines them, and at another it separates them. It puts the most diverse things before the eyes.[45]

This passage seems to support Gentile's interpretation, since fantasy apparently guides man into a religious and transcendent sphere where the divine is to be found. But two points should be made. Firstly, Vico explains fantasy in a manner which makes it impossible to understand the notion as a medium through which man ascends to God in a spiritual way; or that fantasy is a means used by God to control man as a historical individual. Secondly, an interpretation of 'fantasy' in Vico's first oration must take into consideration the fact that he relates this faculty to the ability of producing metaphors, and this ability results in quite a different experience of unity than the one Gentile presentst; the unitary form of this experience is not transcendent, but empirical and social. Before exploring these two points, I shall examine what Vico understands by 'fantasy' in this first oration.

Unfortunately, Vico does not provide any full description of his theory of knowledge in this oration, but only hints at it. He does mention sensation, fantasy, acuteness, memory and ingenuity.[46] The definition of fantasy which Gentile picks up on—the ability to produce mental images and to combine them into new forms—is given by Vico immediately after his treatment of the senses. The senses transmit sense impressions to fantasy, which forms mental images out of these impressions. This relationship between sensation and fantasy is apparently the same as described in *De sapientia*. Vico does not give an explicit analysis of fantasy and its relation to memory, as he does in *De sapientia*, but he does mention memory among epistemological faculties.[47]

But Vico does refer to another faculty, the "highest power in the human intellect", called *facultas percipiendi*, apprehension, which is able to "combine and separate in a swift and acute way".[48] This ability seems to be ascribed to fantasy, but Vico also calls *facultas percipiendi* the most divine faculty of the human mind; yet both fantasy and ingenuity are described as "divine" so *facultas percipiendi* may be either of them.[49] In *De sapientia* the expression *facultas percipiendi* is also used in his definition of the art of topics; here he claims that this art guides the *facultas percipiendi*, which is synonymous with ingenuity.[50]

Corsano has pointed out that even though *facultas percipiendi* literally means faculty of perception, that is, perception through the senses, it should not be understood as such. Instead, it must be understood as a perception of the intellect; it signifies a faculty which receives and forms exterior perception in the human mind.[51] Therefore, Vico calls it "the first perception of the mind"; a "perception", which contains an abundance of inferences, but also a form of perception which is disregarded by philosophers. Vico describes the function of *facultas percipiendi*, apprehension, in the following way:

> In fact, how acute apprehension is! How cleverly it combines and divides! How rapidly it reasons! How many and how rapid the thoughts, faster than my words, which are provoked in each of you when I put forward a metaphor, which pleases Aristotle very much, calling the drinking bowl 'the shield of Bacchus'. This is so, because each of your first see Mars at one side and Bacchus at the other side; then the shield is looked upon at one side, the drinking bowl at the other side. And then, right away, you associate Mars with the shield, Bacchus with the drinking bowl, and you see Mars armed with the shield, Bacchus holding the drinking bowl. At this stage you place in these four images according to their proper positions: Mars and Bacchus in their celestial ones, the drinking bowl and the shield in their terrestrial ones; after this,

considering the particular situations on earth, you realise the
reason for the relations and ponder the specific purpose,
whatever it is that of the shield or that of the drinking bowl;
the purpose of the shield is to keep away enemies, while the
purpose of the drinking bowl is to keep away thirst.
Thereupon, this simile follows; just as Mars uses the shield,
Bacchus uses the drinking bowl, the former to keep away
enemies, the latter to keep away thirst. Furthermore, you
compare the figure of the shield with the figure of the drinking
bowl, and you notice that they both belong to the class of
round objects. At this moment you exchange the four images;
first you attribute the drinking bowl to Mars on the left, then
you attribute the shield to Bacchus on the right; finally you
understand that the shield is the drinking bowl of Mars, and
that the drinking bowl is the shield of Bacchus.[52]

It is indeed remarkable that, in this very passage where he explains the
mind's apprehension, Vico does not use traditional epistemological
terms to describe the highest part of the human mind, but instead
underlines the epistemological process involved in the creation of
metaphors. Vico takes his example from Aristotle's *Poetics*.[53] But what
we do not find in Aristotle is a description of the epistemological process
which takes place in the creation of metaphors. Vico refers to metaphors
extensively throughout his writings, but he never offers such a precise
description again, for which reason the passage is worth attention.[54]

Through the *facultas percipiendi,* man understands the metaphor
"the drinking bowl is the shield of Bacchus". Apprehension combines a
linguistic image depending upon four known signs—Bacchus, Mars,
drinking bowl and shield; at almost the same time it identifies the
ontological *loci*, to which these signs may refer. After this, it is
recognised that the metaphor evokes two specific situations, one in
which the bowl keeps thirst away, and the other where the shield keeps
enemies away. Finally, an identification between the round form of both
shield and drinking bowl allows the specific metaphor to be created,
since it is recognised that this similarity of the signs (roundness)
corresponds to a semantic similarity (to keep something away). At the
centre of this epistemological process we find a "double vision"
combining the four signs freely, and imagining possible associations to

these signs. Furthermore, this "double vision" is multidimensional; it is able to interrelate signs as if they were autonomous, and during this process of combining freely, specific relations between signs are compared with corresponding relations between situations. I call it "multidimensional", because this epistemological process does not proceed from any fixed perspective—on the contrary, it is a playful negation of any pre–established perspective which relies upon a one–dimensional way of conceiving of reality.

This does not mean that this metaphorical reasoning involves no perspective: Vico states that the faculty in question, apprehension, is able to judge in one glance whether or not a perspective is striking and apt. Given the background of the example quoted above, it is obvious that this "judgement" considers the relation between things and their signs, *res et verba*, and not the signs alone. Nevertheless, judgement does not proceed from a logical category, but from an aesthetic one, i.e. the ability to gauge in one glance whether or not something is "ugly" or "deformed".[55] The same idea is expressed in *De sapientia*, where Vico claims that ingenuity's cognition is basically a cognition of "beautiful relations", for which reason he identifies the act of understanding with an act of recognition of beauty.[56]

Comparing this analysis with Gentile's, two conclusions can be drawn. Firstly, in the first inaugural oration Vico does not state anything about a spiritual ascent resulting in an experience of a "unity" beyond sensation, the Plotinian experience of *The One*. On the contrary, Vico describes how human beings are capable of understanding and articulating an empirical and social experience, precisely through fantasy and ingenuity. Secondly, Vico's statement, that man's soul is an image of God,[57] may be interpreted in another way than that of Gentile, as a causal relation between God and man, where God controls man through providence: Vico's statement can also be interpreted as drawing an analogy; the essence of God and that of man is mental activity. As Vico says, "God is always very active; the human soul is similarly always enterprising."[58] God's activity results in the continuous creation of the universe; that of man in the arts. Vico concludes: "Finally, God is the creator of nature, while the soul—if I may say so—is the creator of the arts."[59] If man is understood as an *artifex* of the arts, parallel to God as the *artifex* of nature, the first inaugural oration turns out to be in agreement with the description of fantasy given in *De sapientia*, where it is also said that fantasy is the capacity which makes man similar to God.[60]

I think it is, therefore, reasonable to consider 'fantasy' and 'apprehension', as they are presented in the oration of 1699, as being in agreement with Vico's theory of knowledge from *De sapientia*, dating from 1710. This means that Gentile's idealistic interpretation of 'fantasy', in the oration of 1699, has to be rejected.

The concept of fantasy was also used in *Scienza nuova seconda*, and here one finds that it has the same epistemological meaning as in the two earlier texts, a faculty of forming empirical experience.[61] But in this work it is also possible to find another meaning of this concept, hinted at in the first inaugural oration and strongly interpreted by Gentile; the capacity of so–called primitive people to create ideas about heroes and gods.[62] In 1911, Benedetto Croce interpreted 'fantasy' according to the latter meaning, as the strongest support for his idealistic interpretation of Vico's aesthetics; he interpreted 'fantasy' as the medium through which *Lo Spirito* manifests itself.[63] According to Croce, Vico's aesthetics is therefore idealistic—a notion echoed in Croce's own aesthetics, *Breviario di estetica*. Therefore, when Gentile understands 'fantasy' as a means of communicating with a transcendental reality, he may be influenced by Croce and his reading prejudiced.

On the other hand, if Gentile's idealistic interpretation is rejected, the problem still remains of explaining the dualistic relation between soul and body, which, as noted by Gentile, seems to build upon a Neoplatonic tradition. In 1956, Corsano pointed out that Cicero's *Tusculan Disputations* were one inspiration to Vico's first inaugural oration, thereby questioning Gentile's reading.[64] In fact, Vico himself makes mention of Cicero as the inspiration of the basic idea of the inaugural oration—that knowledge of man's essence, i.e. his soul, is the highest motivation for studying.[65] Corsano has subsequently been supported by Visconti's critical edition of 1975 of this first inaugural oration, which shows that Vico's text is often very close to Cicero's *Tusculan Disputations* and sometimes Vico even quotes directly from this book.[66]

In general, Vico only refers to the first book of these disputations by Cicero, where it is discussed whether or not death is an evil and a hindrance to a happy life. Inspired by Plato, Cicero answers that the soul has a divine origin and does not undergo any destruction or change after death. In other words, the soul is eternal and not dissolved when the body dies and dissolves. Therefore, death cannot be an evil. Visconti notes that Vico's dualistic description of the relationship between soul and body, parallel to the relationship between God and nature, is inspired by Cicero, who had stated that the soul is immaterial but controls the body, just as god is immaterial and controls nature.[67] Hence, Gentile might be wrong when he says that Vico had picked up this psycho–physical idealism from the Neoplatonists of the Renaissance—it certainly could be found elsewhere, and Vico seems to have done so.

How does Vico use Cicero's theory of the relation between body and soul? Cicero had explained knowledge as a recollection of the knowledge which the soul possessed before being deposited in the body, an explanation Cicero may have taken over from Plato, whose dialogue the *Meno* Cicero mentions to support his view.[68] Indeed, Vico makes mention of Plato's dialogue the *Meno* too, praising it for its display of man's capacity of spatial imagination,[69] but he totally ignores the doctrine which was crucial in the epistemology of Plato and Cicero, the doctrine of recollection; instead, he points out sensation, fantasy's ability to shape sense impression, and the power to create metaphors, articulating an empirical experience.[70] Although Vico speaks of memory in terms typical for the Platonic tradition, as "the treasury of the mind",[71] he does not conceive of these "treasures" as Plato had done, namely as a recollection of prenatal knowledge; but as an abundance of relations between thoughts and expressions, *res et verba*, relations which he explains in an empiricistic manner.[72]

In conclusion, it is true that Vico uses Plato's doctrine on the relation between soul and body as a framework for his first inaugural oration, but he makes use of it in his own peculiar way; the divineness of the soul is not due to its recollecting, but to its metaphorical reasoning. As noted by Garin, there is something more than Ciceronianism in this early speech of Vico; there is also an eulogy of metaphorical reasoning, which is totally absent in Cicero's *Tusculan Disputations,* and among the Neoplatonists. Where did Vico then find his inspiration?

4. Tesauro on Metaphor

Vico could have found this inspiration in the literary and philosophical reflection on metaphor, ingenuity and acuteness among the Italian literary mannerists of the previous century. Emanuele Tesauro held an important position during this epoch because of his *Il cannocchiale aristotelico*, first published in 1654. He was the most read of the mannerists, and his books were published in several editions throughout the seventeenth century. Tesauro sets forth a doctrine on metaphor, based on the assertion that the elements in a metaphor correspond to Aristotelian categories, and that man's reasoning should be regarded as an associative linking between such elements. Therefore, metaphors are not literary ornamentation, but forms of thought. On that basis, Tesauro characterises ingenuity, the faculty which reasons through metaphors, in the following manner:

> Natural ingenuity is a marvellous force of the intellect, comprising two natural capacities: perspicacity and versatility. Perspicacity is the ability to penetrate into the most distant and minute circumstances of any subject, such as substance, matter, form, accident, attribute, causes, effects, purposes, sympathies, similar, superior, inferior, signs, definite nouns and synonyms, all of which lie entangled and hidden in any subject matter, as we shall say in its proper place.
>
> Versatility is the ability to compare rapidly all these things, with one another or with the subject matter: it relates or separates them, it extends or diminshes them, it deduces one from another, it hints to one by means of another, and with wondrous skill it replaces one with another, as do the jugglers in their calculations. And this is metaphor, the mother of poetry, of symbols and of *imprese*. And, as we shall see, he who is able to grasp and connect the most remote things, is the most ingenious maker of *arguzie*.[73]

This definition of ingenuity as the ability to identify similarities between remote things, is, of course, similar to the definition of Peregrini and

Vico. Tesauro, however, mentions a series of Aristotelian categories under the heading of 'perspicacity', and, compared with Peregrini, Tesauro operates with a much more ambitious concept of ingenuity, since he considers of metaphorical reasoning as similar to the scientific form of thought, the syllogism, which likewise works through these Aristotelian categories. Tesauro goes on to define metaphor accordingly:

> Finally, we have reached the summit of ingenious figures, step by step, in comparison with which all the other figures considered so far lose their merit, since metaphors are the most ingenious and acute, the most rare and wondrous, the most jolly and valuable product of human intellect. Truly an extremely ingenious product; if ingenuity consists in connecting together distant and separated ideas of the subject matter (as we said), then this is exactly the task undertaken by a metaphor, and by no other figure: drawing the mind, no less than the word, from one genus to another, it expresses one concept through another very different one, and thus finds similarity in dissimilar things. Therefore our author concludes that the making of metaphors is the labour of a sharp and most lively mind.[74] As a consequence, metaphor is the most acute figure of all, since the other figures are formed in an almost grammatical manner, and stop at the surface of a word, while a metaphor, in a thoughtful manner, penetrates into and examines the most abstruse notions in order to combine one with another; and while the other figures dress up concepts with words, metaphor dresses up words themselves with concepts.[75]

Tesauro has a highly original idea of the nature of metaphor. As I have already suggested, he regards metaphor as a form in which it is possible to draw conclusions from the relation between genera and species of metaphors, just as in the syllogism. But, these genera and species which Tesauro presents, are not those of scientific discourse, as in the Aristotelian syllogism, but rather those of everyday discourse.

He regards metaphor as a rhetorical figure, but he isolates it from other rhetorical figures, because it interrelates distinct concepts, contrary to harmonic figures, which only possess harmony in the expression, and to pathetic figures, which only evoke emotions.[76] Of particular interest is

Tesauro's explanation of the recognition of similarity which is involved in metaphors. He says:

> First of all, I notice that metaphors of similarity are well defined and celebrated by him [Aristotle]. They are called "transference from one species to another" and "from one genus to another". Here, using his favourite example, an example of transference from one species to another, could be if you called the shield "Mars' drinking bowl"; or, if you called the drinking bowl "the shield of Bacchus". For the drinking bowl and the shield are two species categorized similarly, under the same genus of round things, as two sisters deriving from the same father in the following manner:

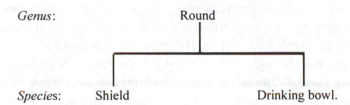

> *Genus*: Round
>
> *Species*: Shield   Drinking bowl.

> This is so, since your fecund ingenuity allows you to "misuse" the name belonging to one species as a name of another one, corresponding to it, since they are directly subjected to the same unambiguous genus.[77]

The crucial point is that Tesauro here asserts what Vico later on states in his first oration of 1699: Vico presents the same epistemological condition for establishing a relation of similarity between Bacchus' drinking bowl and Mars' shield: the discovery of "the round" as a common feature of the shield and the drinking bowl. It seems plausible that Vico's description of this reasoning is inspired by Tesauro; in both, association of separate ideas is mediated by similarities in the signs expressing these ideas. Vico refers to the same notions in his *Institutiones oratoriae*, although he does not mention Tesauro by name, but Peregrini, who assigned to style the same cognitive potential as we have seen in Tesauro.

Both Peregrini and Tesauro hold that discovery of connections between separate ideas is brought about through discovery of similarities in the signs expressing those ideas. Peregrini is concerned with language, Tesauro with images, which means that the discovery of similarities between signs happens in two different ways; for Peregrini, it is crucial to find similarities in the phonetic features, but for Tesauro, one finds visual similarities in the images. Nevertheless, they both argue that the invention of new relations between ideas takes place through a stylistic element, namely *elocutio*. Vico follows this manneristic idea about the cognitive potential of style in his first oration of 1699. Metaphor is, therefore, more than ornamentation of thought. It is the very form of thought, an insight pointed out by Tesauro some decades earlier.[78]

As I said at the beginning of this book, in 1941 Nicolini argued that Vico's *Institutiones oratoriae* mostly contained "popular definitions and divisions, repeated innumerable times and often with the same formulations by Vico—definitions and divisions from countless schoolbooks, published and in the form of manuscripts, from the seventeenth and the eighteenth century." Accordingly, Nicolini cuts out these "popular definitions" in Vico's *Institutiones oratoriae*, including the definitions of metaphor and in particular the above–mentioned example with Bacchus and Mars.[79] This editorial principle was, of course, in accordance with the idealistic interpretation given by Gentile, according to which Vico's early years were philosophically unimportant. But unfortunately it is also a principle which has hindered an understanding of Vico's assimilation of mannerist theories of rhetoric and epistemology.

It thus seems plausible that Vico picked up Tesauro's theory about the epistemological process taking place in the creation or understanding of metaphors. Furthermore, Tesauro offers another way of interpreting Vico's words about the "divineness" of the human mind, which, as shown above, Gentile interprets in an idealistic manner. Vico said that the human mind is divine because it is immaterial but controls matter, namely the body. This is like God, who is immaterial but controls all matter. Tesauro points out another similarity between God and the human mind:

> It is not, therefore, without reason that ingenious men were
> called divine; because, just as God creates *ex nihilo*, an

ingenious person makes being out of non–being. He turns a lion into a man and an eagle into a city; he grafts a woman onto a fish and makes a mermaid into a symbol for an adulator. He combines the upper part of a goat with the tail of a serpent, and makes a chimera a hieroglyph for 'madness'. For which reason some of the ancient philosophers called ingeniousness a sparkle of the divine mind, and others a gift sent from God to his beloved.[80]

Here Tesauro claims that the production of metaphors is what makes man a godlike being; man creates metaphors *ex nihilo*. That man's divineness stems from this is precisely what Vico advances in his first oration of 1699; the inventiveness of man's ingenuity, producing metaphors among other things, is parallel to God's creation of the world.

As has been said, Vico's theory of knowledge is presented as a basis for his reinterpretation of the art of topics. However, what is the relevance of mannerism to this reinterpretation? Mannerist theories on style and reasoning do matter to Vico's idea of topics, since Vico does not repeat the traditional, and practically self–evident conception of topics, a checklist of various *loci* to be investigated; instead, he works out a theory about the epistemological preconditions for the discovery of relevant *loci*, namely a plastic mind able to "see" and "make" unnoticed similarities between different ideas or experiences—exactly the faculty which Peregrini and Tesauro had praised in their aesthetics. Vico's thought about topics is, however, partly an answer to Descartes' method, in which an alternative to the classical topics is presented. I shall, therefore, outline this method of Descartes before returning to Vico's conception of topics.

Notes

1   Vico, *De sapientia, Opere* I, pp. 174, 179.
2   *Ibid.*, p. 177: "An igitur, quia antiqui Italiae philosophi opinati sint mentem humanam nihil percipere nisi per sensus, ut Aristotelaei."
3   *Ibid., Scienza nuova seconda, Opere* IV, § 363: "Nihil est in intellectu quin prius fuerit in sensu."
4   Aristotle, *On the Soul* 432a. See Nicolini, *Commento storico alla seconda 'Scienza nuova'*, note to Vico, *Opere* IV, § 363. See also Mooney, *Vico in the Tradition of Rhetoric*, pp. 225ff.
5   Koch, *Den europæiske filosofis historie*, p. 139.
6   Vico,*Vita, Opere* V, p. 16.
7   See Gregory, *Scetticismo ed empirismo. Studio su Gassendi*, pp. 74–77.
8   Vico, *De sapientia, Opere* I, p. 175: "Nam, si sensus facultates sunt, videndo colores, sapores gustando, sonos audiendo, tangendo frigida et calida, rerum facimus."
9   *Ibid.*, "Phantasia certissima facultas est, quia dum ea utimur rerum imagines fingimus."
10 This aspect can be found in *Oratio* IV from 1704 (Vico, *Opere* I, pp. 37f). Later on it is repeated several times: in *De constantia iurisprudentis* from 1721: "Cumque natura ita comparatum sit: ut qui sensu praenimio et acri phantasia res percipiunt, ii mente puriore parum intelligant et omnia sentiant animo perturbato..." (Vico, *Opere* II, p. 369); in a letter to Gherardo degli Angioli, dating from 1725: "...fortemente immaginarli e quindi vivamente sentirli" (Vico, *Opere* V, p. 195). See also below in the same letter, p. 199).
11 Letter to Gherardo degli Angioli: Vico, *Opere* V, p. 199.
12 *De sapientia, Opere* I, p. 178. See Pareyson, "La dottrina vichiana dell'ingegno", pp. 354–356.
13 *Ibid.* See also Vico, *Polemiche, Opere* I, p. 212.
14 *Ibid., De ratione, Opere* I, p. 81.
15 Aristotle, *Nicomachean Ethics* 1140b; *ibid., Rhetoric* 1378a.
16 Vico, *De sapientia, Opere* I, pp. 175f.
17 *Ibid.*, p. 179: "'Ingenium' facultas est in unum dissita, diversa coniungendi."
18 *Ibid*, p. 185: "Phantasia ingenii oculus..."
19 Mooney, *Vico in the Tradition of Rhetoric*, p. 152.
20 Vico, *De sapientia, Opere* I, p. 179.
21 *Ibid., Vita, Opere* V, p. 34: "E i latini la 'natura' dissero 'ingenium', di cui è principal proprietá l'acutezza."
22 *Ibid., De sapientia, Opere* I, p. 179: "...quid aptum sit, quid deceat, pulchrum et turpe..."
23 *Ibid.*, "...ut Deus sit naturae artifex, homo artificiorum Deus."
24 *Ibid., Institutiones oratoriae*, ed. Crifò, pp. 26f: "Ingenium sit ad excogitandum acutum, ut quam celerrime, et in rei, qua de agitur, medullas penetret, et omnia quae ad rem spectant circumspiciat, colligat, suaeque causae feliciter applicet eique feliciter uniat. Idem sit ad explicandum facile, ut in sententiis res, in verbis sententiae pellucidius vitro perspiciantur; sit et versatile, quodque ad iocos, ad seria, ad lenia, ad aspera, ad facilitatem, ad vim, ad grandia, moderata, tenuia Proteo citius convertatur."

25 Plato, *Republic* 441d, 444d; *ibid.*, *Gorgias* 503e–504e.

26 Vico, *De sapientia, Opere* I, p. 179.

27 *Ibid.*, *Scienza nuova seconda, Opere* IV, § 331.

28 See Löwith, "Vicos Grundsatz: *verum et factum convertuntur*. Seine theologische Prämisse und deren säkulare Konsequenzen", pp. 6, 13f, 16, 32.

29 Vico, *De sapientia, Opere* I, p. 131.

30 *Ibid.*, p. 132: "Scire autem sit rerum elementa componere."

31 *Ibid.*, *Polemiche, Opere* I, pp. 235, 255. See Corsano, *G. B. Vico*, p. 102.

32 Vico, *De sapientia, Opere* I, p. 131: "Altrinsecus, uti verba idearum, ita ideae symbola et notae sunt rerum: quare quemadmodum legere eius est, qui colligit elementa scribendi, ex quibus verba componuntur; ita intelligere sit colligere omnia elementa rei, ex quibus perfectissima exprimatur idea."

33 *Ibid.*, pp. 131f.

34 *Ibid.*, *De ratione, Opere* I, p. 85: "Geometrica demonstramus, quia facimus; si physica demonstrare possemus, faceremus." See also *ibid.*, *De sapientia, Opere* I, p. 176.

35 *Ibid.*, *De sapientia, Opere* I, pp. 175f. See also Pareyson, "La dottrini vichiana dell'ingegno", p. 365.

36 Vico, *Oratio* I, *Opere* I, p. 9: "Vis vero illa rerum imagines conformandi, quae dicitur 'phantasia...'" Compare *ibid.*, *De sapientia, Opere* I, p. 175: "Phantasia certissima facultas est, quia dum ea utimur rerum imagines fingimus." See Corsano, *G. B. Vico*, pp. 28–30. Regarding 'fantasy' and its role in relation to metaphor, see Vico, *Oratio* I, *Opere* I, pp. 19f.

37 Gentile, *Studi vichiani*, pp. 29–35, 40–64.

38 *Ibid.*, pp. 19f. Gentile refers to Vico's statement in *Vita, Opere* V, pp. 31f.

39 Gentile, *Studi vichiani*, p. 20.

40 *Ibid.*, pp. 29–35, 50–52.

41 Vico, *Oratio I, Opere* I, p. 8: "Ut enim Deus per ea, quae facta sunt atque hac rerum universitate continentur, cognoscitur; ita et animus per rationem, qua praestat, per sagacitatem et motum, per memoriam et ingenium divinus esse percipitur. Expressissimum Dei simulacrum est animus. Ut enim Deus in mundo, ita animus in corpore est. Deus per mundi elementa, animus per membra corporis humani perfusus; uterque omni concretione secreti omnique corpore meri purique agunt. Et Deus in mundo, et in corpore animus ubique adest, nec usquam comprehenditur: Deus enim in aethere movet sidera; in aëre intorquet fulmina, in mari procellas ciet, in terra denique cuncta gignit; nec coelum, nec mare, nec tellus Dei circumscriptae sunt sedes: mens humana in aure audit, in oculo videt, in stomacho irascitur, ridet in liene, in corde sapit, in cerebro intelligit: nec in ulla corporis parte habet finitum larem. Deus complectitur et regit omnia, et extra Deum nihil: animus, ut cum Sallustio loquar, 'rector humani generis, ipse agit atque habet cuncta, neque ipse habetur'. Deus semper actuosus: semper operosus animus. Mundus vivit quia Deus est; si mundus pereat, etiam Deus erit: corpus sentit quia viget animus; si corpus occidat, animus tamen est immortalis." Gentile quotes this passage in *Studi vichiani*, pp. 44–46.

42 Gentile, *Studi vichiani*, p. 55: "A sui ad Dei cognitionem ascensio." This statement stems from Vico, *Oratio I, Opere* I, p. 11: "...a sui ad Dei cognitionem graditur et ascendit."

43 Gentile, *Studi vichiani*, pp. 45f.

44 *Ibid.*, pp. 52–54.

45   Gentile brings this quotation in *Studi vichiani*, p. 52. It comes from Vico, *Oratio I*, *Opere* I, p. 9: "Vis vero illa rerum imagines conformandi, quae dicitur 'phantasia', dum novas formas gignit et procreat, divinitatem profecto originis asserit et confirmat. Haec finxit maiorum, minorumque gentium deos; haec finxit heroas; haec rerum formas modo vertit, modo componit, modo secernit; haec res maxime remotissimas ob oculos ponit..."

46   Vico, *Oratio I*, *Opere* I, pp. 8f.

47   *Ibid.*, *De sapientia*, *Opere* I, p. 178; *Oratio I*, *Opere* I, p. 8.

48   *Ibid.*, *Oratio I*, *Opere* I, p. 9.

49   *Ibid.*, p. 8: "ingenium divinus"; *ibid.*, *Opere* I, p. 9: "...quae dicitur 'phantasia', dum novas formas gignit et procreat, divinitatem profecto originis asserit et confirmat."

50   *Ibid.*, *De sapientia*, *Opere* I, p. 180; *Polemiche, Opere* I, pp. 201, 271.

51   Corsano, *G. B. Vico*, p. 30.

52   *Ibid.*, *Oratio I*, *Opere* I, pp. 9f: "Etenim facultas illa percipiendi quam acris ! illa componendi, secernendique quam solers ! ratiocinandi illa quam velox ! Dum tralacionem, quam tantopere commendat Aristotles, profero, et vini pateram 'Bacchi clypeum' appello, quot et quam celeres motus in cuisque vestrum dicto citius excitari. Videt enim quisque vestrum primo hinc Martem, hinc Bacchum; deinde hinc clypeum, hinc pateram intuetur. Statim illico Martem cum clypeo, Bacchum cum patera componit, et Martem armatum clypeo, Bacchum gestantem pateram cernit; ibi tum e regione quodque sua, Martem et Bacchum superna, pateram et clypeum inferna confert; atque illico, terrae locos omnes percurrens, ab illo caussarum desumit finem, et cum clypei tum paterae proprios usus considerat, illius hostes, huius autem sitim arcere; et continuo similitudinem adhibet, quod uti Mars clypeo, ita Bacchus patera utatur, ille ut hostes, hic vero ut arceat sitim; et praeterea clypei pateraeque figuras confert, easque in genere rotundarumque rerum congruere animadvertit! Hinc extemplo transversum graditur, et has quatuor formas decussat; et sinistrorsum prius Marti pateram, dextrorsum deinde Baccho clypeum appingit, ut postremo clypeum pateram Martis, pateram clypeum Bacchi esse cognoscat."

53   Aristotle, *Poetics* 1457b.

54   See Corsano, *G. B. Vico*, p. 29.

55   Vico, *Oratio I*, *Opere* I, p. 10.

56   *Ibid.*, *De sapientia*, *Opere* I, p. 179.

57   *Ibid.*, p. 8: "Expressissimum Dei simulacrum est animus."

58   *Ibid.*: "Deus semper actuosus; semper operosus animus."

59   *Ibid.*: "Tandem Deus naturae artifex; animus artium fas sit dicere, Deus."

60   *Ibid.*, *De sapientia*, *Opere* I, pp. 175–176. See also Corsano, *G. B. Vico*, pp. 29f.

61   Vico, *Scienza nuova seconda*, *Opere* VI, § 699.

62   *Ibid.*, §§ 3, 6, 375.

63   Benedetto Croce, *La filosofia di Giambattista Vico*, p. 47.

64   Corsano, *G. B. Vico*, pp. 26–28.

65   Vico, *Oratio I*, *Opere* I, p. 7.

66   In *Bollettino del centro di studi vichiani*, nr. 3, 1975, pp 4–39: Giambattista Vico, *Oratio I*.

67   Visconti assigns this passage from Vico's *Oratio* I, "...uterque omni concretione secreti omnique corpore meri purique agunt." (Vico, *Opere* I, p. 8), to Cicero's *Tusculan Disputations*, 1.66, which Visconti quotes in the following way: "animorum nulla in terris origo inveniri potest. nihil enim est in animis mixtum

atque concretum, aut quod ex terra natum atque fictum esse videatur [...]. singularis est igitur quaedam natura atque vis animi, seiuncta ab his usitatis notisque naturis. [...]. nec vero deus ipse, qui intellegitur a nobis, alio modo intellegi potest nisi mens soluta quaedam et libera, segregata ab omni concretione mortali." See Vico, *Oratio I*, ed. Visconti, l. 128–129.

68   Cicero, *Tusculan Disputations* 1.57. Plato's doctrine on recollection: *Meno* 82a–85e; *Phaedo* 72e–77a.

69   Vico, *Oratio I*, *Opere* I, p. 13.

70   *Ibid.*, p. 9.

71   *Ibid.*, p. 12: See Augustine, *Confessions* 10.8.

72   Vico, *Oratio I*, *Opere* I, p. 12.

73   Tesauro, *Il cannocchiale aristotelico*, pp. 32f: "L'ingegno naturale è una maravigliosa forza dell'intelletto, che comprende due naturali talenti: perspicacia e versabilità. La perspicacia penetra le più lontane e minute circonstanze di ogni suggetto, come sostanza, materia, forma, accidente, propiretà, cagioni, effetti, fini, simpatie, il simile, il contrario, l'uguale, il superiore, l'inferiore, le insegne, i nomi propri e gli equivochi: le quali cose giacciono in qualunque suggetto aggomitolate e ascose, come a suo luogo diremo.

La versabilità velocemente raffronta tutte queste circonstanze infra loro o col suggetto: le annoda o divide, le cresce o minuisce, deduce l'una dall'altra, accenna l'una per l'altra, e con maravigliosa destrezza pon l'una in luogo dell'altra, come i giocolieri i lor calcoli. E questa è la metafora, madre delle poesie, de' simboli e delle imprese. E quegli è più ingegnoso, che può conoscere e accoppiar circonstanze più lontane, come diremo."

John A. Goodall defines *impresa* in "Impresa", p. 149, as a "personal or familial badge or device comprising a design accompanied by an apt word or brief motto suggesting in veiled terms its significance".

74   *Ibid.*, *Poetics* 1459a.

75   Tesauro, *Il cannocchiale aristotelico*, p. 73: "Ed eccoci alla fin pervenuti grado per grado al più alto colmo delle figure ingegnose, a paragon delle quali tutte le altre figure fin qui recitate perdono il pregio, essendo la metafora il più ingegnoso e acuto, il più pellegrino e mirabile, il più gioviale e giovevole, il più facondo e fecondo parto dell'umano intelletto. Ingegnosissimo veramente, però che, se l'ingegno consiste (come dicemmo) nel ligare insieme le remote e separate nozioni degli propositi obietti, questo apunto è l'officio della metafora, e non di alcun'altra figura: perciò che, traendo la mente, non men che la parola, da un genere all'altro, esprime un concetto per mezzo di un altro molto diverso, trovando in cose dissimiglianti la simiglianza. Onde conchiude il nostro autore che il fabricar metafore sia fatica di un perspicace e agilissimo ingegno. E per consequenza ell'è fra le figure la più acuta: però che l'altre quasi grammaticalmente si formano e si fermano nella superficie del vocabulo, ma questa riflessivamente penetra e investiga le più astruse nozioni per accoppiarle; e dove quelle vestono i concetti de parole, questa veste le parole medesime di concetti."

76   *Ibid.*, p. 88.

77   Not to be found in Raimondi's edition, and so I quote the one published in Halle in 1664: Tesauro, *Il cannocchiale aristotelico*, pp. 331f: "Primieramente da lui trov'io riconosciute, & celebrate alcune metafore di simiglianza: chiamate METAFORE DA UNA SPECIE ALL'ALTRA: & DA UN GENERE ALL'ALTRO. Da una Specie ad altra sarà (secondo il suo favorito esempio) se tu chiamilo *Schudo*, TAZZA DI MARTE. Overo la *Tazza*, SCUDO DI BACCO.

Peroche la *Tazza*, & lo *Scudo*, son due *Specie* similmente collocate sotto al medesimo Genere di COSA RITONDA: come due Sorelle procedenti dal medesimo Padre in questo modo:

Genere: RITONDO

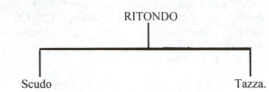

Specie: Scudo   Tazza.

Talche ti è permesso dal tuo fecondo ingegno, di abusar del Nome di una Specie, per il nome di un'altra, collaterale: soggiacente al medesimo Genere Univoco, & Immediato."

78   See Briscia, "L'arguta et ingegnosa elocuzione", p. 57; Raimondi, "Ingegno e metafora nella poetica del Tesauro", pp. 1–4, 7f.

79   By comparing Nicolini's edition with Crifò's, it turns out that Nicolini has ignored the three following definitions, all quoted from Vico's *Institutiones oratoriae*, ed. Crifò, § 37, p. 294: "'Similitudo' est 'ita Bacchus patera propellit sitim, ut Mars clypeo propellit hostes'. 'Icon' autem est 'Bacchus patera, tamquam clypeo sitim'. 'Metaphora' vero est 'Bacchi clypeo sitim propellamus.'" ("'Similarity' is 'Bacchus conquers thirst with the drinking bowl as Mars the enemies with the shield'. But 'a simile' is 'Bacchus conquers thirst with the drinking bowl, as if it was a shield'. And truly 'metaphor' is 'we conquer thirst with the shield of Bacchus.'")

80   Tesauro, *Il cannocchiale aristotelico*, pp. 32f: "Però che, sì come Iddio di quel che non è produce quel che è, così l'ingegno di non ente fa ente, fa che il leone divenga un uomo e l'aquila una città. Inesta una femina sopra un pesce e fabrica una Sirena per simbolo dell'adulatore. Accoppia un busto di capra al deretano di un serpe e forma la Chimera per ieroglifico della pazzia. Onde fra gli antiqui filosofi alcuni chiamarono l'ingegno particella della mente divina, e altri un regalo mandato da Iddio a' suoi più cari."

Chapter Four

Vico's Discussion of Descartes' Idea of Topics

1. Descartes' Methodology

René Descartes brings us from Italy to France, where Petrus Ramus (1515–1572) had presented new ideas concerning logic and rhetoric, hoping to solve the methodological problem of Scholasticism, namely how to establish an inventive logic.[1] Descartes recognised the value of Ramus' endavour, and in *Discours de la méthode* he tried to find a solution to the same problem. But this was not the immediate purpose of the work. *Discours* was published in 1637 as a preface for three essays on optics, geometry and meteorology. These essays were extracts from Descartes' compositions on physics, *Le Monde* (The World), which he had hesitated to publish because of the condemnation of Galileo Galilei (1564–1642) and his heliocentric theory, presented in 1633 in *Dialogo sopra i due massimi sistemi del mondo: tolemaico, e copernicano* (Dialogue Concerning the two Great Theories of the Universe, the

Ptolemaic and the Copernican), one year before Descartes' *Discours*. According to Descartes himself, he would risk a similar conviction by publishing *Le Monde*, because he had indirectly affirmed Galilei's astronomical theory. The purpose of *Discours* was, therefore, to change the attitude of the Inquisition in order to make a future publication of *Le Monde* possible without the same risk of condemnation.[2]

Discours is, in itself, too condensed and obscure to elucidate Descartes' methodology. But in his unfinished and posthumous work *Regulae ad directionem ingenii* (Rules for Guidance of the Mind) we find further elaborations on the rules stated in *Discours*. Since neither Vico nor his contemporaries knew this Latin text, and since it is not the scope of my book to treat Descartes' methodology *per se*, but only to suggest how it became crucial to Vico's reflections about topics, I shall confine this discussion to the parts of *Discours* which are of relevance to this point.

Discours is a remarkable personal work. In it, Descartes looks back on his own search and scientific investigation—a telling feature, inasmuch as its methodology is strongly influenced by his own needs, especially for intellectual certainty. It was written in 1636 in Holland, where Descartes had settled in 1629, and it includes his first years as a schoolboy at the Jesuit school of La Flèche, from 1606 up till 1614. The education which Descartes received at La Flèche was organised according to Jesuit pedagogical precepts, as stated in *Ratio studiorum* (Organisation of Studies). According to Descartes, this early teaching was decisive, because it motivated him to study literature. These studies lasted six years, and they included courses in Latin and Greek grammar, history, poetry and rhetoric.[3] He claims that others had persuaded him to believe that through this study he would attain "a clear and certain knowledge about everything useful in practical life".[4] Gilson notes that the Jesuit teachers at La Flèche would hardly have said such a thing; instead, Gilson assumes that it is reminiscent of the Renaissance.

Whatever the case, Descartes was disappointed. Certainly, studies in grammar and history could offer some knowledge of the past and its customs, but he could not help thinking that those studies also make the student estranged from his own time.[5] Furthermore, he held that ancient myths mislead students into believing in impossible things—

a criticism which he also applies to the study of history, since its *exempla* may lead people astray from right conduct for the same reason. Not only was he disillusioned with grammar and history, but also with poetry and rhetoric. He certainly liked these disciplines—he even claims that he had a passion for poetry and literature—but he thought that the talent of writing poetry and of eloquent speech was an innate gift, impossible to acquire through studying. In relation to rhetoric, he claims that it has a rational basis, since he who guides his reasoning in the best possible manner, i.e. in a logical manner, will always be good at persuading others. Only phonetic mistakes which slip into the speech will hinder this.[6]

According to *Ratio studiorum,* rhetoric is taught during the forth year, where the students read Cicero in particular, but also Sallust and Livy. If Descartes has Cicero's reflections on rhetoric in mind, then even a simple comparison will reveal quite a difference between Descartes' view of the orator and Cicero's: Cicero defined the task of the speaker as threefold, to teach, move and please; Descartes reduces the task of the speaker to one, to teach, that is, to construct logical proof in a valid way.[7] Evidently, Descartes overlooks the fact that a speaker is always treating an issue which is characterised by uncertainty, where rational thought is insufficient, as Cicero claimed.

Descartes' doubts concerning the value of the study of history and its *exempla*, and his rationalistic conception of rhetoric, may be understood in the light of an early influence of Stoicism, especially Seneca's *De vita beata* (On the Good Life), which Descartes read at La Flèche, and which influenced him deeply according to Gilson.[8] Seneca had rejected the *exempla* of history as well as its *sensus communis*, because they mislead man and oppose reason, which ought to guide man to a happy life.[9] Although Descartes states that he rejected the philosophy which he encounted on La Flèche, seing it as nothing but "an endless disputation of opinions",[10] and although he claims to have doubted all opinions in his search for certainty later on, he still seems to have taken up Stoic views.[11] The Stoic inspiration is in part epistemological, in part ethical. The epistemological influence appears in the expression first used in *Discours,* "le bon sens", which is a translation of the Stoic notion *bona mens*, found in Seneca's *De vita beata*, which signifies the ability of reason to discern truth form falseness.[12] The ethical inspiration underlies *Discours*; within Descartes' new method it is impossible to lay down any moral rules, because this field is lacking certainty. He therefore works out a so–called provisional morality, valid until logically undeniable rules for moral conduct are established without prejudice or haste. One of the maxims of this provisional morality states that one should not desire external things, only the internal, i.e. thought, because external things are beyond man's control.[13] The wish for self–sufficiency, obtained by not desiring the external world which is under the command of fortune, was an important doctrine in Seneca's thought.

Descartes never found in these subjects the degree of certainty he was striving for, so he gave up hope of finding it in the most important disciplines of humanism with its *studia humanitatis*.[14] Instead, he decided only to search "within himself" and in "the great book of the world", by which he meant that he would confront the consequences of his own decisions, which he had abided by during his travels.[15] These travels lasted from 1616 to 1618. In this way he hoped it was possible to avoid what he considered to be the lack of practical consequences of humanistic studies. But neither did the study of "the great book of the world" give him any certainty—only empirical evidence for the relativity of morality and confused powers of reason. Having arrived at this point, his second attempt to obtain certainty in his moral conduct had failed, since it remained a crucial condition to possess powers of reason which enabled him to judge correctly.[16]

The turning point came in 1619 when Descartes was twenty–three. He conceived of the idea of a common method for apodictic and probable sciences.[17] The distinction between probable and apodictic sciences goes back to Aristotle's *Nicomachean Ethics*, where he distinguishes the unchangeable world, field of the apodictic sciences, from the changeable world, field of the probable sciences. Apodictic sciences are characterised by a degree of exactness and necessity which allows a demonstrative proof to have logical necessity. Probable sciences, on the other hand, treat the probable which does not allow the same strict logical inference. Instead, it is possible to make use of practical wisdom, known as *phronesis*.[18] The purpose of this division was to adapt the scientific method to the scientific object, not to demand a higher degree of exactness than the object would allow.[19] Descartes' intention was to work out a common method to these radically different scientific fields, where mathematics, an apodictic science itself, was regarded as the scientific ideal and as a general methodological basis.[20] Precisely how mathematics could offer such a wondrous method was not clear at once to the young Descartes. In his unfinished work *Regulae ad directionem ingenii*, dating from 1628, the method is established in the form of twenty–one rules, and in *Discours*, from 1637, these rules are reduced to four.

The four rules in *Discours* are formulated in the imperfect tense, and not in the present, which might have been more suitable to the rules of a method. The reason may be that Descartes wanted to connect the validity of the method with the correctness of the concrete scientific results, which the method had given rise to, and which were presented subsequently in *Discours*. But it did not take long before Descartes convinced himself that the method possessed a general validity and that it might even be regarded as a universal method.[21] Descartes states in the first rule:

> The first was never to accept anything for true which I did not clearly know to be such; that is to say, carefully to avoid precipitance and prejudice, and not to comprise more in my judgement than what was presented to my mind so clearly and distinctly as to exclude all reason of doubt.[22]

Here Descartes presents a criterion for the object of scientific reasoning. Firstly, he demands that only that which appears in a clear manner to the mind, can be accepted as true. This "clarity" is ascribed to that which immediately appears true. It is opposed to conjunction, which does not immediately appear true. By demanding clarity, Descartes takes a decisive step which he had thought of already at La Flèche, namely not to allow any graduation between truth and falsity, between absolute certainty and ignorance.[23] Consequently, the probable field of science is excluded, since its premises are disputable, and nothing but the apodictic field can be subjected to scientific reasoning.

In order to exclude those scientific fields which ought to be excluded, Descartes elaborates this general demand for clarity. Firstly, judgement should be suspended until clarity has been attained. Secondly, judgement should not be based on preconceived ideas. Thirdly, judgement should not include more than what appears clearly and distinctly to the mind. By "clearly" Descartes means that the idea must actually be present in the process of reasoning, and as such immediately evident. The opposite he calls "obscure". The demand for momentary recognition means that previous ideas, which were experienced with such "clarity" and which are still considered as such in memory, cannot be regarded as clear ideas, but as clear and obscure ones. In the quotation above it is also said that the idea should be conceived "distinctly". By "distinctly" is meant that the idea should not include foreign elements, that is, be separated from other ideas. The opposite is the "confused".[24] If the idea is clearly and distinctly conceived, it will appear in a manner where its truth cannot be doubted.

When Descartes comments on this rule, it turns out that the kind of clarity he has in mind is the clarity characteristic of mathematics.[25] By pointing out the clarity particular to mathematics as the criterion of truth, Descartes turns against the above–mentioned Aristotelian principle, and against this principle as a Scholastic doctrine. For the Scholastics claimed that the formal character of mathematics gives it a certain solidity and clarity, but this degree of certainty cannot be found in the sciences treating material objects.[26] In the first rule, then, Descartes is not as concerned with how to reason scientifically as much as he is concerned with the proper object of science. His vision of a unitary science is, therefore, a reduction of science to those fields which are characterised by the kind of certainty found in mathematics. In contrast to Descartes, Aristotle strove to provide the field of the probable, an uncertain field, with a scientific method, namely topics, intended as a method to carry out discussions, based on probable premises, without self–contradiction.[27] According to Aristotle, the ethics of individuals and communities should be discussed on the basis of such premises, and the dialectical reasoning, guided by the art of topics, was consequently of utmost interest to the speaker intending to discuss social issues.[28] Seen from this perspective, Descartes' first rule is a violent attack, not only on humanistic studies such as history, poetry and rhetoric, which are all concerned with man's conduct, in one way or another, but on the whole field of probable sciences.

Descartes goes on to claim that in order to reason with this degree of clarity, the obscure and confused must be eliminated through an initial analysis. Accordingly, in the second rule Descartes prescribes an analysis which breaks down the problem into the smallest possible parts; in the third rule he prescribes a synthesis of these broken down parts, beginning with the simple and uncompounded and moving towards the compounded; in the fourth and last rule he endorses a complete survey to be worked out in order not to ignore anything.[29] It is difficult to understand fully these last three rules from *Discours*, because of their vagueness: what kind of "smallest possible parts" should be a result of an analysis? What did he mean by a deduction from "the simple to the compounded"? How would it be possible to attain a complete survey of a problem, given the fact that this lack of any possible overview is part of the problem?

Nevertheless, Descartes obviously understood the four rules as constituting a logical system, which was a generalisation of the procedure he had used earlier with success within mathematics, and also as a logical system which could serve as an alternative to the logic of the Scholastics. Descartes claims—like other intellectuals of his time—that the logic of the Scholastics is nothing but a method of expounding ideas already discovered, not a method of discovering new ideas. Furthermore, he criticises their logic for being so vague in its notions, that even ignorance passed unnoticed.[30] Descartes explains that in his mathematical research he had discovered a procedure capable of solving mathematical problems hitherto unsolved, and of discovering ignorance about other mathematical problems, which is, of course, a precondition to any solution of a problem.[31] His ambition was to incorporate this inventive element into logic, thus providing a method adaptable to all other fields of science.[32]

Descartes wanted to apply two branches of mathematics to logic, namely geometry and algebra. Until Descartes' time, these two branches had existed separately as branches of pure mathematics, and, Descartes adds, without any real value to physics, because of this separation:

geometry, that is, Euclidean geometry, was dependent upon man's contemplation of spatial figures, which, according to Descartes, was an obstacle for understanding; algebra, on the other hand, was so dependent upon its own strange nomenclature that it hindered one's reason from making use of it.[33] Descartes had attained impressive results within mathematics by combining these two branches into an algebraic geometry, where spatial figures are replaced by algebraically expressed relations. He wanted to incorporate this algebraic geometry into his own logic, to be precise, in the second and the third rule.[34]

The criterion for clear ideas meant immediate recognition of the truth of a proposition. In order to reach this kind of knowledge, an initial analysis had to be undertaken, prescribed in the second rule. The analysis offered by the syllogistic argumentation, is explained step by step, from premises to conclusions, for which reason this form of analysis cannot meet with Descartes' demand for instant recognition. But according to Descartes, geometry can offer such a form of proof, and apart from granting immediate recognition, it allows one to discover new ideas.[35] In other words, this algebraic geometry, also called the geometrical method, was a new inventive logic, a true *ars inveniendi*.[36] The synthesis, prescribed in the third rule, should start from the uncompounded, and step by step move towards the compounded. In order to keep the propositions as distinct as possible during this analysis, and at the same time instantly cognizable, he applied algebraic symbols, that is, letters, to the parts and to their mutual relations, which he had previously analysed; in this way it was possible to compare several relations at the same time.[37]

Descartes' geometrical method did meet with the widely felt need for an inventive logic. Ramus had tried to solve this problem a century earlier, but it was Descartes' solution which became influential in the science of the following centuries. The art of topics and its fortune is closely connected with the rise of this new Cartesian method. Traditionally, topics had been a means of inventing or discovering truths, but according to Descartes, the geometrical method is capable of this without help from any topics. If Descartes did not directly state this, then Antoine Arnauld and Pierre Nicole certainly did so in their book *La logique ou l'art de penser* (Logic or the Art of Reasoning). It was published for the first time in 1662, and its system better known as the "Port–Royal Logic", which combined Descartes' method with Aristotelian logic. In this book Arnauld openly declares that the traditional topics was useless, and that the task of this art, namely to discover truths, could be fulfilled by the geometrical method.[38] This was the problem for Vico, who asked whom to belive: Arnauld and his geometrical method, or Cicero and his traditional topics?[39]

2. Vico's Rejection of the Cartesians

Vico believed neither Arnauld nor Cicero. Instead, he elaborated his own ideas about method and topics. Descartes had published *Discours* in 1637, ten or fifteen years before the most important publications of Peregrini and Tesauro, but Descartes had presented his ideas in the dialectically oriented climate of France, far away from the Italian humanism where rhetoric was still central. Vico did not, therefore, encounter Descartes' *Discours* and *Meditationes* before 1702, a few years after he had returned to Naples from his stay at Vatolla, where Vico had studied important humanists, such as Lorenzo Valla (1405–1457), and where he had assimilated Italian literature and philosophy.[40] Furthermore, he had taught rhetoric at the university at Naples for three years.[41] In other words, Vico had just finished the kind of studies in language, mythology, history, rhetoric and poetry which were condemned by Descartes, when Descartes' anti–humanism came into vogue in Vico's native city.

Vico calls the new method *nova critica*, or just *critica*, referring to Descartes' geometrical method and its application within logic and rhetoric, undertaken by Arnauld and Nicole in *La logique ou l'art de penser*.[42] But sometimes Vico simply regards Descartes' and Arnauld's works as one single method with the analytically deductive element as a common feature.[43] Before I move on to Vico's well–known criticism of Descartes' rationalism, I shall call attention to the genealogy of Vico's idea of ingenuity, which is central to Vico's criticism.

In 1708 Vico held an inaugural oration with the title *De nostri temporis studiorum ratione* (On the Study Methods of Our Time), which was published in an extended version the following year.[44] Although Vico had criticised, in *De ratione*, the methodology of Descartes on the basis of his theory on ingenuity, it is important to bear in mind that Vico did not elaborate his concept of ingenuity in opposition to Descartes, but from the rhetoric of mannerism, thereafter using it in his criticism of Descartes. Already in his first inaugural oration of 1699, almost a decade before *De ratione*, Vico had stressed the role of ingenuity and its epistemological potential in relation to metaphors, largely inspired by Tesauro. This idea of ingenuity, and its capacity to produce new perspectives through metaphors, is also present in *De ratione*, although it is subordinated to the general, methodological discussion.[45] Vico's *Institutiones oratoriae* of 1710–1711, and in particular § 35, is the first place where he reveals his dependence on mannerist rhetoric. Vico's concept of ingenuity was, therefore, initially inspired by mannerism, and later elaborated and applied to a methodological discussion. This is why I have discussed *Institutiones oratoriae* before *De ratione*, although the former is chronologically later than the latter.

The first rule in Descartes' method recommends that one only regard an idea as true if it possesses the exactness and truth of an apodictic idea. Vico puts forward the objection which has already been stated, that in this way Descartes excludes the field of the probable.[46] Vico also points out that human beings have an uncertain nature and a free will, for which reason their ethical behaviour cannot be explained on the basis of apodictic premises, that is to say, it cannot be treated scientifically within Descartes' narrow idea of science. He thus opposes Descartes' methodological monism with the pluralistic one of Aristotle, according to which probable sciences—social sciences and rhetoric— should be cultivated as though parallel to apodictic sciences.[47] This is Vico's methodological alternative to Descartes' method, in which ethics, social sciences and rhetoric are excluded, and only mathematics and natural science regarded as scientific fields.

But Vico's objection to Descartes' methodology goes even further. Vico's rehabilitation of probable sciences, especially rhetoric, is also a rehabilitation of the special faculty of cognition which is vital to understanding or sensing social life in its organic form, namely *sensus communis*, which was discarded by Descartes in *Discours*. This faculty is vital to man as a social individual, and, consequently, to the speaker as well. Vico lays stress upon this faculty, because a discussion within the probable sciences has to obtain some of its premises from the actual *sensus communis*; such discussions cannot depart from a priori and abstract premises, as Descartes suggests in his method.[48] Therefore, Vico considers Descartes' rejection of probable sciences as a threat to elementary capacities valuable to man as a social and ethical being. Vico's methodological objection against Descartes thus marks an epistemological, and in particular ethical revolt against a possible consequence of Descartes' rationalistic methodology: the isolation of individuals within a rational, social atomism.[49]

Enough has been said about Vico's criticism of Descartes' method in relation to the probable sciences. But even when Descartes' geometric method is considered in relation to apodictic sciences, e.g. physics, Vico is still critical. He refutes Descartes' claim of a high degree of exactness within physics, because, as he says: "We are able to prove geometrical truths because we have invented geometry; only if we had created physical matter, would we be able to prove its truths."[50] This principle—later known as the *verum et factum* principle[51]—has an important consequence for the method of physics: man cannot understand nature, since he has not created it; the only way to obtain knowledge in physics is, therefore, through empirical observation, which allows for a more or less qualified hypothesis. Descartes, on the other hand, wants to base physics on an a priori analysis of clear and distinct ideas; Vico rejects this procedure and suggests a method in which empirical observations, and suitable combinations of these, are crucial. The opposition between Vico and Descartes is radical. Descartes wants to discard sensation totally, thus making abstract and rational analysis possible; Vico insists on the primacy of sensation, and he ascribes to rationality the more humble role of discovering concrete relations between individual observations. This discovery calls for a capacity to synthesise, but according to Vico, it is hindered by Descartes' method, about which Vico makes the following assertion:

> The geometrical method prescribes that discussions about physics are carried out in brief terms, as in geometrical demonstrations, and with ornamentation prohibited. Therefore, you will see that modern physicians have a dry and rigid manner of discussing: in physics of this sort, both before

> and after it has been learnt, a proposition must always be
> deduced from one which precedes it; this hinders the ability of
> listeners to discern similarities between different ideas, as is
> characteristic to philosophers. This ability is regarded as the
> source and chief part of any acute and elegant expression.
> Quibbling (*tenue*) is not the same as acuteness (*acutum*), since
> the quibble follows one line, the acute two. The most
> prominent position among acute remarks (*dicta acuta*) is taken
> up by metaphor, which marks the highest distinction and most
> important ornament of any expressive speech.[52]

Central to this passage is the relationship between the style of scientific discourse, which must be without ornaments according to Descartes, and scientific reasoning, or the ability to see similarities, which is, according to Vico, hindered by the geometrical method. The ability to see similarities is described as the work of ingenuity in Vico's *Institutiones oratoriae*, where he regards it as a cognitive faculty interrelating ideas through similarities of expression, and where precisely this faculty is regarded as the source of scientific recognition.[53]

Another affinity between the quotation above and *Institutiones oratoriæ,* is that in the latter Vico conceives of reasoning as taking place through an aesthetic category; likewise, in the quotation above, he describes scientific recognition in literary terms, *ornatus et acutus,* ornate and acute. Furthermore, he determines metaphor in *De ratione* just as he had done in his *Institutiones oratoriae,* as the most suitable form of expression of ingenuity. Moreover, in *De ratione* he describes metaphor as *acuta et ornata*: The aptitude of a metaphor to express acute reasoning, *acutus,* is opposed to dry and quibbling reasoning, *tenuis*; the first follows "two lines", the last "one line". Vico returns to this description in *De sapientia* and in his autobiography, clarifying that the reasoning which follows "one line" corresponds to the deductive method in Descartes' analysis of clear and distinct ideas, contrary to the reasoning following "two lines", which corresponds to the analogical reasoning of ingenuity.[54]

At this point we should recall the importance of the multidimensional character of metaphorical reasoning. Vico claims that such a plurality of perspectives depends upon a linguistic sensibility and its ability to combine the expressions of ideas in a free and precise way. In this way, stylistic sensibility and metaphorical operation become vital to the analogical reasoning with which Vico seeks to confront Descartes' one–sided rationality in *De ratione*. Metaphorical rationality is thus an alternative to Descartes' one–sided, logically deductive rationality; not an irrational alternative, but one where rationality is given a much broader definition, and where language is understood as central to reasoning itself.

According to Vico's *Institutiones oratoriae*, phonetic material, and the mental images evoked by it, are crucial to the discovery of relations between ideas. This conception is to be found in *De ratione*, where Vico says that French makes reasoning dry and referential, because of its abundance of substantives, while Italian is more suitable for metaphorical reasoning, since it is rich in mages.[55] From a linguistic point of view this opinion can hardly be taken seriously, inasmuch as Vico admits in his autobiography that he gave up learning French.[56] But from a philosophical point of view the idea is interesting: Vico concludes in *De ratione* that "ingenious persons are created by language, not language by ingenious persons".[57] No other language than French is thus able to "produce" a geometrical analysis, which is dry and stripped of images. When considering Vico's views here, it is hard to imagine a more radical disagreement with Descartes' and Bouhour's instrumental conception of language.

Vico's objections to Descartes' algebraic geometry, as expressed in *De ratione* and in his autobiography, must be seen in relation to his theory on metaphor.[58] Vico does not alltogether reject geometry, but only the algebraic version which Descartes elaborated, because it had an unexpected pedagogical consequence, namely that Euclidean geometry was neglected in the schools, in favour of Descartes' algebraic geometry. According to Vico, the geometry of Euclid, also named the synthetical geometry, trains man's spatial imagination, giving him the ability to discover truths and their interrelations: "to discover something new is the office of ingenuity; true geometry trains ingenuity."[59] Accordingly, Vico does not accept Descartes' algebraic and analytic geometry, since by leaving out mental images it excludes spatial imagination; it does not allow ingenuity or fantasy any material to work with, thereby excluding the ability to think.[60]

The disagreement is obvious. Descartes regards the bonds between thought and spatial imagination as an obstacle to reason, while Vico sees these bonds as vital to reason. In his criticism of Descartes' algebraic geometry, Vico is thus defending the epistemological potential of metaphorical reasoning and its imagery, which also played a significant role in Aristotle's theory on *asteion* and in the aesthetic theory of the mannerists.[61] Vico admits, however, that Descartes himself had worked out his method, in which images are rejected, in an ingenious way employing an abundance of imagery. Unfortunately, Descartes' disciples were too obedient to his idea of a rationality without figurative imagination.[62] Therefore Vico's criticism of Descartes' method may concern the new method of the Cartesians, *demonstratio more geometrico*, rather than Descartes himself.

On a pedagogical level Vico warns against the algebraic geometry of Descartes, since it will hinder children from learning what children learned in antiquity through Euclidean geometry, namely to use their ingenuity, to think. According to Vico, each age has its own advantages, and teaching ought to be adapted to this phenomenon; while adults have a well developed reason, children possess a lively imagination.[63] Vico states that the geometry of Descartes "blinds fantasy, weakens memory, makes ingenuity lazy and hinders understanding". Instead, Vico suggests that imagination is trained through studies in painting, sculpture, architecture, music, poetry and rhetoric, and memory is developed through studies in language and history.[64] Here Vico is the conservative one, demonstrating his loyalty to the pedagogical ideal of humanism in his rejection of Descartes, who had devalued studies in history, poetry and rhetoric.

After these objections to Descartes' methodology and their pedagogical consequences, Vico turns to Arnauld's logic. His discussion of Arnauld and Descartes does not focus on the rather trivial and self-evident issue of whether or not truths should be discovered before they can be explained, but considers how these truths should be discovered. Vico comments on Arnauld's popular logic with these words:

> Nowadays, only *critica* is celebrated; it is not that *topica* precedes it, but rather that it is completely neglected. This is wrong, because just as discovery of arguments precedes judgement of their validity, *topica* should be prior to *critica*.[65]

Indeed, Arnauld had rejected the traditional topics as a means of discovering the material of the syllogism, but instead he had inserted Descartes' geometrical method to discover that material. Arnauld claims that this method of Descartes can serve as a much more fertile art of topics. Therefore, Vico is not quite fair in this treatment of Arnauld. Nevertheless, Vico identifies Arnauld's logic with *critica*, one of the two notions which form the dichotomy *critica–topica*. The meaning of these two notions is explained in *De sapientia*, at the point when Vico refers to Cicero's *Topica*, where Cicero distinguishes between two disciplines within logic: one discipline is concerned with the discovery of arguments, *ars inveniendi*, and the other one is concerned with the judgement of the validity of arguments, *ars iudicandi*. *Topica* corresponds to *ars inveniendi*; *critica* to *ars iudicandi*.[66] According to Cicero, *topica* is a means towards *inventio*, and must precede *critica*, which Vico affirms.[67] Inspired by Cicero, Vico thus criticises Arnauld for not paying attention to the discovering of arguments, only to the arranging of them. Consequently, Vico repeats the criticism which Cicero made of the Stoics; Arnauld reduces his logic to an *ars iudicandi*. Vico wants to unite *topica* with *critica*, since "*critica* makes our speech true, while *topica* makes it rich in arguments".[68]

3. Vico Defines the Art of Topics

Vico thus presented an ideal relation between the art of topics and the art of judgement in *De ratione*, dating from 1708. In the following years he elaborates his idea of topics and its epistemological implications. As I have pointed out, Vico stated in *Institutiones oratoriae* that the acuteness of ingenuity is the real force in topics. In autumn 1710 Vico published *De sapientia*, where he offers decisive clarification of the epistemological aspects related to his original idea of topics.

In *De sapientia* Vico advances an etymology which reveals an original conception of the art of topics and that of judgement. Human cognition, Vico says, consists of three parts, and to each of them corresponds a discipline: Apprehension, *facultas percipiendi*, is guided by the art of topics; judgement of such apprehensions, *facultas iudicandi*, by the art of judgement; interrelation of ideas, *facultas ratiocandi*, by the method of reasoning.[69] Vico hereby gives the traditional idea of topics a twist, since it was understood as a purely technical method for the speaker, a checklist presenting various aspects to seek in order to discover arguments; Vico does not regard topics as such a mechanical and exterior means, but as a theory of cognition, as an empirical logic, guiding man's inventive apprehension. This radical move towards a theory of cognition astonished the critics who took note of it in *Giornale de'letterati d'Italia*, and Vico was consequently forced to explain his original conception, to which point I shall return.[70]

Arnauld had audaciously declared that Aristotle's *Topics* was useless. Although Vico approves of Arnauld's statement, he does not agree with Arnauld's conclusion, that traditional topics should be substituted with the algebraic geometry of Descartes;[71] instead, Vico seeks to develop the traditional topics, thus hoping to turn it into a truly inventive method. As in his *Institutiones oratoriae,* he claims that if the inventor's cognition is "penetrating", then even the Aristotelian list of topical places will be a useful starting point, not only in rhetoric, but also in natural science.[72] The problem is, of course, how cognition works in a "penetrating" way.

If the role of the traditional art of topics is to discover a middle term in a syllogism, then Vico's topics must similarly explain how there can be discovered a "mediating" similarity between different ideas or experiences, to which the mediated terms refer. The faculty discovering such similarities is ingenuity: "Ingenuity is the faculty by which man is capable of understanding the similar, and of making it similar."[73] This idea is close to that of Cicero, who had argued that the checklist of traditional topics is insufficient in helping the speaker discover relevant arguments; only the speaker's acuteness, *acer ingenium*, is capable of discovering those arguments.[74] Vico picks up this idea of Cicero, but goes on to highlight the faculty of seeing similarities between different ideas or experiences as the important ability in the kind of ingenuity about which Cicero wrote.

These "similarities" are not obvious to the person investigating, but must be recognised or determined as such by that person himself; he must be able to make "the given" given to himself. On this point Vico's general theory of knowledge is interesting for at least two reasons: firstly, here fantasy is the faculty which forms sense impressions into mental images; secondly, ingenuity works out a linguistic unity which expresses various ideas or experiences, an active and critical process. The material for Vico's topics, presented in *De sapientia*, is both actual and previous experiences—the last class existing in memory and subjected to the forming of fantasy, like actual sense impressions. Therefore, Vico claims that fantasy is "the eye of ingenuity".[75] This relation between topics, fantasy and ingenuity makes it clear that although I have called Vico's topics an "empirical logic", it does not mean that it is regarded as an art which guides sensorial perception; it guides the intellectual perception, the interrelating of ideas in the mind, although these ideas derive from sensation. Therefore, despite Vico's empirical position, he does not regard the mind as an instrument of truth, but as its source.

Having established this idea of topics, he relates it to the history of philosophy. He ascribes the plastic power of discovering similarities between widely different ideas to all philosophy preceding Aristotle, characterising this manner of reasoning as "inductive". Socrates was the last philosopher who reflected in this way; Aristotle, the Stoics, and later on Descartes, all modified their reasoning according to the syllogism or the sorites, through which radical differences cannot be connected, only what is already considered as similar and homogeneous: the individual under species, species under genus.[76] The syllogism and the sorites force the intellect to follow an ontological scheme and to deduce truths according to the hierarchical structure of the scheme. This uninventive application of an already existing perspective, implicit in the ontological scheme of Aristotle, is analogical to Descartes' logcially deductive method, and Vico thus identifies the geometrical method of Descartes with the sorites of the Stoics. The alternative is the inductive way of thinking, which relates ideas across ontological schemes, thus connecting what is regarded as heterogeneous.[77] This idea of induction may be even more radical than that of the philosopher Francis Bacon (1561–1626);

Bacon demanded that the objects for induction be ordered into ontological categories before the act of induction, which may conceal a hidden deduction.[78]

Vico's idea of induction, however, is very similar to his idea of metaphor, which is likewise characterised by an interrelating of different things. This conception of metaphor was also that of Aristotle, who had explained metaphor as a semantic transformation from one ontological category, or individual, to another. Peregrini stressed this characteristic of metaphor, produced by ingenuity, stating that ingenuity differs from the intellect; the latter interrelates ideas which have a "natural relationship", that is, ideas related according to an ontological scheme; but the former is characterised by composing ways of reasonings which depart from such a scheme.[79] Although Peregrini had defined ingenuity in this flattering way, it had no epistemological consequences, since he had also ascribed to ingenuity non–cognitive status. As shown, Vico opposed Peregrini on this point, ascribing to ingenuity a cognitive value, without which it would be impossible for ingenuity to see the like and to interrelate it through induction.[80] Finally, Tesauro's doctrine on metaphor and metaphorical reasoning may play a role in Vico's praise of metaphor as inductive: like Peregrini, Tesauro had stated that the speaker, who uses metaphors, has the possibility of breaking an ontological scheme.[81] Therefore, metaphor becomes the celebrated form of expression. Nevertheless, one should not forget that Peregrini, Tesauro and Vico presupposed the forms of the syllogism in their theory of metaphor, and one should not overrate their polemical attitude towards the Aristotelian logic, which, ironically, they were to a large extent dependent upon.

Vico's idea of topics was highly untraditional, and he was asked by the critics of *Giornale de'letterati d'Italia* to explain what he meant by calling topics an art guiding cognition, *facultas percipiendi*, and not just a traditional checklist. Vico replies:

> You claim that "topics is the art of discovering causes and arguments in order to prove something; until now, no topics has existed, which provides rules for us about how to control and direct well the simple impressions in our mind".

> But *I* really do define topics in this way; "argument" within this discipline does not signify the "order of the proof", as it is commonly understood and which the Latins call "argumentatio" [an adducing of proof]. Instead, you should understand that third idea which you discover in order to relate the two ideas in the issue at hand, and which is called the "middle term" in the schools; therefore, topics is the art of discovering the middle term. But I want to expand this: this is the art of apprehending in a true manner, since it is the art of discerning, assisted by all the topical places related to the issue discussed, everything to be found in it, so we are able to distinguish properly and obtain an adequate concept about the issue. This is so, because falseness of judgements derive from one sole reason, that the ideas more or less precisely represent the subject matter; consequently, we cannot be certain, unless we are prepared to examine the issue thoroughly by means of all the questions which we are able to pose.[82]

In this quotation a middle term and two mediated terms are mentioned: the two mediated terms, which are parts of the major and the minor premises in a syllogism, must be united through a third term, the middle term. Clearly, Vico accepts the common definition of topics as an art of discovering the middle term, but he adds that topics must also treat the cognitive precondition for discovering such a middle term; the true relations between ideas about a given subject matter, "the art of apprehending in a true manner". This conception of topics will provide an "adequate concept" to the investigator.

The phrase "adequate concept" is a typical rationalistic notion, but Vico does not use it as the rationalists did, as applying to clear and distinct ideas which possess the exactness of mathematics. Among the rationalists, the usage of this concept is confined to the apodictic sciences. It is, therefore, peculiar that Vico uses the term in his topics, which is primarily a method for the complementary, scientific field of the probable. Aristotle had thus introduced his *Topics* with these words: "The purpose of the present treatise is to discover a method by which we shall be able to reason from generally accepted opinions about any problem set before us..."[83] According to Aristotle, topics is a method which can be applied within the probable sciences, where we are forced to argue from "generally accepted opinions"—a fundamental conception of topics which is certainly to be found in Cicero and Vico too. The rationalists, on the other hand, would label such "opinions" as "inadequate ideas". Vico is thus polemical in his use of the term, not only because he uses it in the field of the probable, but also because he uses it about a kind of cognition which derives from sensation, which the rationalists regard as nothing but "inadequate ideas".[84]

As has already been said, Vico's idea of topics is basically a means for directing human apprehension, *facultas percipiendi*. This original conception is also to be found in the quotation above, where topics is "the art of apprehending". Vico also used the concept *facultas percipiendi* in his first oration of 1699; here and in *De sapientia* the concept is used to apply to the mind's apprehension of impressions, and in both texts he regards this faculty as the "first operation of the mind".[85] In the oration of 1699, he determines this faculty as a metaphorical reasoning—a way of reasoning in which stylistic sensibility and creativity plays a crucial role in the discovery of relations between different ideas. Therefore, one may ask whether it is sustainable to interpret Vico's idea of topics as intimately related to his theory of metaphorical reasoning. In fact, when Vico is criticising Descartes' method in *De ratione*, he accuses it for prescribing a formal and closed deductive way of reasoning, and he mentions the metaphorical way of reasoning as an open and inventive alternative; the use of stylish and acute metaphors is not just embellishment of scientific thought, but absolutely vital to the inventiveness of scientific thought.[86]

If these scattered remarks on topics are gathered together, a truely original idea of topics emerges. Cicero considered topics as an *ars inveniendi*, a method of discovery, ingenuity as the ability to make the actual discovery, *inventio*, of topical places. In the rhetoric of literary mannerism, the scope of ingenuity is moved from the level of argumentation to the level of style, and its invention is not primarily concerned with invention of logical arguments, but with forms of expression. Vico developed the insights of the mannerists as regards the epistemological potential which is bound to language, still as pure expression, and he came to see linguistic sensibility as an important element in the invention of ingenuity. But although this kind of *inventio* works through an aesthetic sensibility, its stylistic inventions do not deal exclusively with the form of expression, but with concepts as well. In this way Vico returns to the conception of topics of Aristotle and Cicero—an art of discovering facts about reality—but Vico adds a decisive innovation by explaining how *inventio* may take place through an aesthetic category. Aesthetic fascination thus becomes a central point in Vico's idea of topics.

Enough has been said about Vico's idea about topics until, say, 1712. In this period topics is a guide for the inventions of ingenuity, where these concepts are related to Vico's theory of knowledge. After 1712 these concepts remain important, but they are from now on ascribed a dynamic and inventive role in the development of institutions within human civilisation, described in *Scienza nuova seconda*.[87] His interest in "ingenuity" and "topics" within such a history of civilisation emerges after 1712, immediately following the publication of *De sapientia* and the ensuing polemic. He notes in his autobiography that the subsequent discussion about topics had been honourable, but also that he afterwards came to discard the etymologies advanced in *De sapientia*. Instead, he turned towards "universal etymologies", that is, in lieu of explaining the genesis of man's concrete cognition, he seeks to explain the development of human civilisation in its various cultural forms.[88] This drastic reorientation led to his theories about history of language and, among other things, philosophy of law.

One may wonder to what extent the mannerists' reflections on style, central to his early theories about ingenuity and topics, remain a valuable subtext in Vico's later writings, especially in relation to *Scienza nuova*. Here, he writes:

> But, in this night of darkness where the first and most distant antiquity is hidden, an eternal light appears, never fading away, that says what cannot be denied: that this civilised world has clearly been made by men, and therefore, if ever possible, we can find the principles of this world within the modifications of our own mind.[89]

What did Vico mean by "modifications of our own mind"? How did he conceive of language and thought in his late period? Are there any similarities with the conceptions of his early years? In *Scienza nuova* he describes myths, or to use his expression, *generi fantastici,* as an imaginative reasoning which takes place through poetic species and genera. As has already been said said, Tesauro had stated that man's metaphorical reasoning likewise takes place through poetic species and genera, the only difference being that in *Scienza nuova* Vico uses these poetic species and genera within a phylogenetic perspective, namely the history of civilisation, while Tesauro employs these concepts within a ontogenetic perspective, or man's momentary cognition. The parallel is striking, and Vico's early encounter with mannerist theories on language and symbols may play a hitherto unnoticed role in his major work, *Scienza nuova.*

Notes

1   See Gilbert, *Renaissance Concepts of Method,* pp. 119, 121f; Ong, *Ramus, Method, and the Decay of Dialogue,* pp. 270, 288f, 291; Rummel, *The Humanist–Scholastic Debate in the Renaissance and Reformation*; Mooney, *Vico in the Tradition of Rhetoric,* p. 51.

2   Descartes, *Discours de la méthode,* pp. ix–x. In this section on Descartes' methodology, I am using the information provided by Gilson in the notes to his edition of *Discours,* which is listed in the bibliography.

3   *Ibid.,* pp. 4f.

4   *Ibid.,* p. 4: "....une connaissance claire et assurèe de tout ce qui est utile à la vie..."

5   *Ibid.,* p. 6.

6   *Ibid.,* p. 7.

7   *Ibid.,* p. 5. See Cicero, *De optimo genere oratorum* 1.3.

8   Descartes, *Discours de la méthode,* p. 6.

9   Seneca, *De vita beata* 1.4–5.

10   Descartes, *Discours de la méthode,* p. 8.

11   *Ibid.,* pp. 6, 16.

12   *Ibid.,* note to p. 1, l. 17; 2°: "...Le bon sens..."

13   *Ibid.,* p. 25.

14   Kristeller, "The Modern System of Arts", pp. 174–179.

15   Descartes, *Discours de la méthode,* p. 9.

16   *Ibid.,* pp. 9f.

17   *Ibid.,* pp. 12f.

18   Aristotle, *Nicomachean Ethics* 1139a; 1140b.

19   *Ibid.,* 1094b.

20   Descartes, *Discours de la méthode,* pp. 17, 19.

21   *Ibid.,* pp. 21f.

22   *Ibid.,* p. 18: "Le premier était de ne recevoir jamais aucune chose pour vraie, que je ne la conusse évidemment être telle: c'est–à–dire, d'éviter soigneusement la précipitation et la prévention; et de ne comprendre rien de plus en mes jugements, que ce qui se présenterait si clairement et si distinctement à mon esprit, que je n'eusse aucune occasion de le mettre en doute."

23   *Ibid.,* p. 8.

24   *Ibid.,* p. 18.

25   *Ibid.,* p. 19.

26   *Ibid.,* note to p. 7, l. 24–25.

27   Aristotle, *Topics* 100a.

28   *Ibid.,* *Rhetoric* 1354a, 1355a.

29   Descartes, *Discours de la méthode,* pp. 18f.

30   *Ibid.,* pp. 17f.

31   *Ibid.,* pp. 20f.

32   *Ibid.,* pp. 17, 19.

33   *Ibid.,* pp. 17f.

34   *Ibid.,* pp. 19–21.

35   *Ibid.,* p. 19.

36   *Ibid.* See *Regulae* V, p. 379: "Tota methodus consistit in ordine et dispositione eorum, ad quae mentis acies est convertenda, ut aliquam veritatem inveniamus.

Atqui hanc exacte servabimus, si propositiones involutas et obscuras ad simpliciores gradatim reducamus, et deinde ex omnium simplicissimarum intuitu ad aliarum omnium cognitionem per eosdem gradus ascendere tentemus." From this passage it is clear that the second and third rule in *Discours* were considered as one rule in *Regulae*, and that Descartes understood the algebraic geometry as an *ars inveniendi*, substituting the traditional topic and its form of *inventio*.

37   Descartes, *Discours de la méthode*, pp. 19f.

38   Arnauld, *La logique ou l'art de penser* 3.17; 4.2.

39   Vico, *De ratione, Opere* I, p. 83.

40   Vico relates in his autobiography that he had studied the Aristotelian logician Peter of Spain (1210/1220–1277), and his *Summulae logicales* (Compendium of Logic) at the age of fourteen, and that he had "dissented" from this tedious study, since it was "unsuitable for an ingenious mind like his". A few years later he became interested in Lorenzo Valla—maybe because he was critical towards Aristotelian logic, which Vico had detested at such an early age. See Vico, *Vita, Opere* V, pp. 4f, 8ff. See also Struever, "Vico, Valla, and the Logic of Humanist Inquiry".

41   Vico, *Vita, Opere* V, p. 25.

42   The term applied to Descartes' algebraic geometry: Vico, *De ratione, Opere* I, p. 79; to Arnauld's logic: Vico, *De ratione, Opere* I, pp. 82f.

43   Vico,*Vita, Opere* V, pp. 13f.

44   *Ibid.*, *Vita, Opere* V, p. 32. Battistini claims that the publication of *De ratione* was in the spring of 1709, not 1708, as Vico indicates in *Vita*. See Vico, *Opere*, edited by Andrea Battistini, note 2 to p. 37.

45   Compare Vico, *Oratio I, Opere* I, pp. 9f. with *ibid.*, *De ratione, Opere* I, p. 86.

46   *Ibid.*, *De ratione, Opere* I, p. 81.

47   *Ibid.*, pp. 90, 81.

48   *Ibid.*, p. 86.

49   See letter to F. S. Estevan, 12 January 1729: Vico, *Opere* V, pp. 212–218, in particular p. 214.

50   *Ibid.*, *De ratione, Opere* I, p. 85: "...geometrica demonstramus, quia facimus; si physica demonstrare possemus, faceremus."

51   *Ibid.*, *De sapientia, Opere* I, pp. 131f, 175f; *ibid.*, *Scienza nuova seconda, Opere* IV, §§ 331ff.

52   *Ibid.*, *De ratione, Opere* I, p. 86: "Deinde geometrica methodus physicas dissertationes iuxta ac geometricas apodixes, tamquam contentas doceri tantum, ornari vetat. Itaque recentiores physicos omnes genere disserendi contento ac severo uti animadvertas: cumque haec physica, et cum discitur et cum percepta est, perpetuo ex proximis proxima inferat, eam auditoribus facultatem occludit, quae philosophorum propria est, ut in rebus longe dissitis ac diversis similes videant rationes: quod omnis acutae ornataeque dicendi formae fons et caput existimatur. Neque enim tenue idem est atque acutum: tenue enim una linea, acutum duabus constat. In acutis autem dictis principem obtinet locum metaphora, quae est omnis ornatae orationis maxime insigne decus et luculentissimum ornamentum."

53   *Ibid.*, *Institutiones oratoriae, Opere* VIII, §§ 35ff.

54   *Ibid.*, *Vita, Opere* V, p. 14; *ibid.*, *De sapientia, Opere* I, pp. 179, 184.

55   *Ibid.*, *De ratione, Opere* I, pp. 94f.

56   *Ibid.*, *Vita, Opere* V, p. 22.

57   *Ibid.*, *De ratione, Opere* I, p. 95: "Linguis ingenia, non linguas ingeniis formari..."

58   *Ibid.*, *Vita, Opere* V, p. 14; *ibid.*, *De ratione, Opere* I, pp. 85f.

59   *Ibid., De ratione, Opere* I, p. 87: "Nam nova invenire unius ingenii virtus est: ingenium vero geometria exercet." See also *ibid., Vita, Opere* V, p. 15.

60   *Ibid., Vita, Opere* V, p. 14; *ibid., De ratione, Opere* I, p. 81.

61   See Corsano, "Vico and Mathematics", pp. 430f. See also the letter to Gherardo degli Angioli: Vico, *Opere* V, p. 195.

62   Vico, *Polemiche, Opere* I, p. 275.

63   *Ibid., De sapientia, Opere* I, pp. 177f.

64   *Ibid., Vita, Opere* V, p. 14; *ibid., De ratione, Opere* I, p. 81.

65   *Ibid., De ratione, Opere* I, p. 82: "Deinde sola hodie critica celebratur; topica nedum non praemissa, sed omnino posthabita. Incommode iterum: nam ut argumentorum inventio prior natura est, quam de eorum veritate diiudicatio, ita topica prior critica debet esse doctrina."

66   *Ibid., De sapientia, Opere* I, pp. 269f. See Cicero, *Topica* 1.6.

67   Cicero, *Topica* 1.7.

68   Vico, *De ratione, Opere* I, p. 83: "...ut critica veraces, ita topica nos fieri copiosos..."

69   *Ibid., De sapientia, Opere* I, p. 180.

70   The critics noticed this unusual conception of topics in their first article, *Primo articolo, Opere* I, pp. 201. Vico then defends his idea in *Prima risposta, Opere* I, pp. 212f. This, in turn, made the critics ask for a fuller explanation in *Secondo articolo, Opere* I, p. 228. Vico responded in *Seconda risposta, Opere* I, pp. 268ff.

71   Arnauld, *La logique ou l'art de penser* 3.17-18. See Vico, *De sapientia, Opere* I, p. 182.

72   Vico, *De sapientia, Opere* I, p. 182.

73   *Ibid.*, p. 183: "Ea enim ingenium est, quo homo est capax contemplandi ac faciendi similia."

74   *Ibid.*, p. 186. Vico refers here to Cicero, *De oratore* 2.162–175.

75   Vico, *De sapientia, Opere* I, p. 185. On the relationship between fantasy and memory, see *ibid.*, pp. 177f. See Mooney, *Vico in the Tradition of Rhetoric*, p. 129; Pareyson, "La dottrina vichiana dell'ingegno", pp. 360f.

76   Vico, *De sapientia, Opere* I, pp. 183f. See also *ibid., Scienza nuova seconda, Opere* IV, § 499.

77   *Ibid., De sapientia, Opere* I, p. 184; *ibid., De ratione, Opere* I, p. 86.

78   See Cesare, "Sul concetto di metafora in Giambattista Vico", p. 218.

79   Peregrini, *Delle acutezze*, pp. 122f.

80   See Vico, *De sapientia, Opere* I, p. 179.

81   Tesauro, *Il cannocchiale aristotelico*, pp. 98f.

82   Vico, *Seconda risposta, Opere* I, pp. 268f: "Dite che 'la topica è arte di ritruovare ragioni e argomenti per pruovar che che sia; né mai infino ad ora aver veduto topica veruna, che diaci regole di ben regolare e dirigere le semplici apprensioni delle nostre menti.'

Io pur diffinisco cosí la topica; ma 'argomento', in quest'arte, non suona 'disposizione di una pruova', come volgarmente si prende e da' latini *'argumentatio'* si appella; ma s'intende quella terza idea, che si ritrova per unire insieme le due della questione proposta, che nelle scuole dicesi 'mezzo termine'; talché ella è un'arte di ritruovare il mezzo termine. Ma dico di piú: che questa è l'arte di apprender vero, perché è l'arte di vedere per tutti i luoghi topici nella cosa proposta quanto mai ci è per farlaci distinguer bene ed averne adeguato concetto; perché la falsitá de' giudizi non altronde proviene che perché l'idee ci rappresentano piú o meno di quello che sono le cose: del che non possiamo star certi, se non avremo raggirata la cosa per tutte le questioni proprie che se ne possano giammai proporre."

83 Aristotle, *Topics* 100a

84 In between Descartes' *Discours* and this polemic we find Leibniz' *Meditationes de cognitione, veritate et ideis* (Meditation upon Cognition, Truth and Ideas), published in 1684. Here Leibniz had defined an "adequate idea" as clear and distinct, using Descartes' notions, which could be recognised symbolically or intuitively (pp. 32, 36). Ideas originating from sensation are determined as clear but confused, and are thus called "inadequate" (p. 34). See also Vico, *De ratione, Opere* I, p. 86.

85 Vico, *De sapientia, Opere* I, pp. 180, 183; *ibid., Oratio* I, *Opere* I, p. 10.

86 *Ibid., De ratione, Opere* I, p. 86. Cf. Cesare, "Sul concetto di metafora in Giambattista Vico", p. 221; Vasoli, "Topica, retorica e argomentazione nella 'prima filosofia' del Vico", p. 198; Pöggeler, "Vico e l'idea di topica", p. 75.

87 Vico, *Scienza nuova seconda, Opere* IV, §§ 495, 496.

88 *Ibid., Vita, Opere* V, pp. 37f.

89 *Ibid., Scienza nuova seconda, Opere* IV, § 331: "Ma, in tal densa notte di tenebre onde'è coverta la prima da noi lontanissima antichitá, apparisce questo lume eterno, che non tramonta, di questa verità, la quale non si può a patto alcuno chiamar in dubbio: che questo mondo civile egli certamente è stato fatto dagli uomini, onde se ne possono, perché se ne debbono, ritruovare i princípi dentro le modificazioni della nostra medesima mente umana."

Appendix

A. Extracts from

Matteo Peregrini

ON 'ACUTEZZE', WHICH ARE COMMONLY CALLED LIVELY WITS,
VIVACITIES AND CONCEITS

Chapter I
In which, after the motivation for writing the present treatise has been
indicated, a general exposition of the subject is given. And in which,
having considered briefly what belongs to this subject according to the
authors, the arduous task is pointed out.

Among the depravities which have recently been sneaking in,
contaminating common speech, indiscreet affectedness of *acutezze*,[1]
conceit or lively wit seems to exceed all the other ones. This is a kind of
embellishment more flattering and tickling than any other one, and
therefore it is very powerful in leading to great disappointments the
minds of those who are infatuated by it. Flattery has always been a
mischievous adviser, and the escort of pleasure, when the mighty bridle
of sound judgement does not rein it in, will always be an escort of little
faith. For this reason people nowadays get carried away, right to the
point where they impudently deliver the most obvious lies. And one may
very well say in the words of Quintilian about some of these otherwise
very kind spirits, that "perverseness of judgement leads to the most
detestable absurdities".[2]

Through these persons an idea is introduced which is more
impure and disguised than those unworthy styles which the ancient
rhetoricians used to loath under the label of "childish" and "parentirso",
that is, fanatical. I wish that these vivid and brilliant talents, who run in
this arena with such abandon and in such great number, would observe
what Petronius says on this matter: "With your permission I must tell
you the truth: you teachers have caused the ruin of true eloquence. Your
tripping, empty sounds stimulate certain absurd effects into being, with
the result that the substance of your speech languishes and dies."[3]

For all this I do not condemn them, like all those who lose their way without knowing it; on the contrary, I find them more needy of compassion than blame. And if they do deserve to be pitied and helped, then certainly the tender and noble talents do, who, being inadvertently enamoured of the effulgence of what they think are stars and are nothing but fireflies, innocently run completely off the tracks. For this reason, postponing to a more appropriate occasion the consideration of the other points of criticism which have been indicated to me by my very learned friend Don Vincenzo Renieri in a very courteous letter about the depraved eloquence, I shall treat here separately those points of criticism which are related to the question of *acutezze*.

In order to do so, I intend to pinpoint their nature and attributes, and I shall do my best to put down on these pages all that which appears to me to be appropriate. I shall state my opinion, always prepared to change it if others, by means of a serious discourse, should prove it wrong. In order to examine the nature of the theme in question, I shall presuppose five things as being true and quite evident. Firstly, *acutezza* does not consist in a reasoning, but in a sentence, which may have several parts, but, nevertheless will always be a unity, at least virtually. *Acutezza* is almost a soul, and therefore it can give life only to one body, and not to several separate bodies. Secondly, a saying which is informed by *acutezza* will necessarily belong to the category of beauty and delight. Thirdly, in the field of eloquence, beauty and delight vary extensively to a lesser or greater degree. Fourthly, in this scale of degree, that beauty and delight which are peculiar to *acutezza* leave behind not only the rank of "little", but also that of "mediocre". Finally, *acutezza* does not depend upon the quality of the subject or on the signified object, but on the quality of the artifice and the way of speaking...

Chapter III
In which the essence of 'acutezza' is explained in more distinctive terms.

In order to present more clearly what has been said in the preceding chapter, and to investigate the nature of the wondrous *acutezze* in depth, I shall proceed as follows. In a sentence there is nothing but words, signified objects and their mutual connection. The words as well as the objects or things, which are considered separately, are sheer matter: therefore, *acutezza* is necessarily concerned with the connection. This can apply to the relation between words, between things and words, or between things; and in each case the connection may be with or without style. When the connection is natural or causal or otherwise without artifice, it cannot equally show any problem belonging to our examination, because it is presupposed that an *acutezza* is something stylish. Since the artifice must produce something wondrous, it must not be ordinary, but rather, remarkably rare. And since it must shape an object which is extremely delightful for the mind to look at, its rarity and impressiveness will result from the ability to make a very decorous order to appear between the parts which are joined with style in the sentence. This is obvious, since all the things which, being composed by several parts, are to produce an exceptional delighting object, do so mainly through an extremely suitable correspondence between their single parts. You can tell this by experience in the case of music. And physical beauty—something much beloved by sages and by mutual agreement— is based mainly on rarity of proportions. Therefore, in the connection, which comes from style, both in regard to things and to words, which is to be considered here, the strength must depend entirely on the mutual order of the parts.

The stylistic connection of words with words consists in their mutual arrangement. When this arrangement is stylish, owing only to a decorous order of sounds with sounds or of parts with parts so that the enunciation is distinct and, as we are accustomed to say, harmonious, it cannot pertain to our discussion: because rhythm, even though it is considered by Demeter to be a form of elegance, is, as Cicero said, a very trivial thing and as such one worthy of a rather ordinary mind. But when style consists of a certain symmetry between two parts opposing each other, it may possess some rare degree of considerable *acutezza*. This was also touched upon by Cicero, when he wrote that the oration is harmonious "not only through rhythm", but sometimes "through a certain joining and construction of the words".[4] What this joining may be is pointed out by Cicero himself right below, when he says that it takes place "when similar is placed against similar or opposite against

opposite".[5] This correspondence of parts with parts may be that of
syllables with syllables; that of a word with another word; that of a
clause with another clause, or that of a sentence with another sentence.
Paronomasia[6] and antithesis occupy this field entirely. We may call them
opposition and concord respectively. In any case, it is always somehow
enticing, often childish, and sometimes it has some *acutezza*. For
instance, "Iucundum est amari si curetur ne quid insit amari; Dulcedo
avium ducit ad avium" (It is pleasant to be loved, but we must take care
that there is no bitterness in that love; Wild birds' sweet song leads us
into the wilderness).[7] These are two examples of paronomasia—that is,
examples of a concord based merely on words, quoted from Quintilian;
"rather to be avoided than imitated."[8] Rhyme, which was introduced by
those poets who wrote in the vernacular, derives all its childish charm
from this source. For instance, "Sic vos, non vobis mellificatis apes ;/ sic
vos, non vobis nidificatis aves" (As you, bees, have not made honey for
our sake, so have you, birds, not made nests for our sake)[9] and other
pentameters by Virgil, which are elegant for this reason too. When there
is nothing but paronomasia, the concord will necessarily be something
trivial, and style will not be so marked by ingenuity as to be wondrous.

When the *acutezza* of words is joined with the gravity of things,
which are also made to oppose each other, their elegance may become
manly and efficacy take over in the place of charm. This is the case, for
instance, of sentences such as "reipublicae nec deesse nec superesse
volo" (I wish neither to fail the Republic nor to survive it),[10] as Asinius
Pollio said during the civil wars; or, in Sallust, "Caesar munificentia
magnus habebatur, integritate vitae Cato" (Caesar was esteemed because
of his generosity, Cato for the uprightness of his life),[11] or else what was
said by Caesar marching in Spain against the Pompeian army, before
coming back later on, as he did, to fight Pompeius; "Se ire ad exercitum
sine duce et inde reversurum ad ducem sine exercitu" (To go to meet an
army without a leader, and thereafter to return to meet a leader without
an army).[12] And again, a saying uttered against Caesar when he made
himself a dictator, "Brutus, quia reges eiecit, consul primum factus est;
hic, quia consules eiecit, rex postremo factus est" (First of all Brutus was
consul, since he drove the kings from Rome; since this man drove out the
consuls, he at last is made our king).[13] In these examples one can

observe that the invention of opposition is far from common and that the things advanced in conjunction oppose each other to such an extent that the style reveals a particular force of ingenuity and, as a consequence, it reaches an *acutezza* which is not only verbal, but real and marvellous. Hence, the same can happen in many other sayings of this kind.

The stylish connection of words with things takes place every time the sound or the elocution is judiciously transported from its normal meaning to a foreign one. In this case, yet more things are tacitly related to things, because the thing newly signified will tacitly be connected to that thing which is signified normally—not only because of the term being made common, but also for the reason which made this association possible. This stylish connection can—because of the quality of the words and itself—reach the point where it produces such a rare harmoniousness, that it obviously reveals itself as stemming from a special kind of dexterity.

This happened when Cato, speaking about one who said, after he had used up most of his property in gluttony and finally lost his last house in a fire: "I have done 'sacrifice for the road.'"[14] This was the expression of a sacrifice in which, after having dined well, all the leftovers from supper were burnt, according to habit and rite of religion. The invention of such a befitting comparison through which the word was conveyed from its normal meaning to its new meaning, made such ingenious adroitness shine in the sentence as to make Cato ever since remarkably wondrous. The same holds true in relation to the saying of Augustus, who, asked what had happened to his *Ajax*, answered that "Aiacem suum in spongiam incubuisse" (His Ajax had fallen on his sponge).[15] Augustus had started to compose a tragedy on the story of Ajax, who put an end to his life by letting himself fall on the sword, but since he had not succeeded in putting this plan to effect (luckily, perhaps), he had erased what he had already written: something which was normally done with a sponge. Of this same kind was an *acutezza* which the parasite Cordius said when, sitting at a dining table, he saw one consume a liquid dish in such disgusting manner that he spilled part of it. Cordius said: "you cannot eat and you want to paint."[16] In the first as well as in the second saying, the words, transferred with precise motives, bring about a double connection so cunning that you clearly recognise the work of an adroitness particular to ingenuity. But you will understand this better shortly.

The connection between things also takes place in two ways. One is perceptible, and simply consists in ordering, which, bearing certain correspondences between suitable words, may provide the above–mentioned opposition. The other simply involves order between two things, and through its art it may well sometimes provide a very vigorous elegance as well as efficacy, but never wondrous *acutezza*. An example of vigorous elegance can be found in what Florus said concerning the war of the Romans against Antiochus: "Primum trepidatio, mox fuga, dehinc triumphus" (First there was panic, then flight, and finally triumph).[17] An example of efficacy we can see in Cicero's speech against Verres: "Facinus est vincire civem Romanum, scelus verberare, prope parricidium necare. Quid dicam in crucem tollere?" (To tie a Roman citizen is a crime, to flog him is an abomination, to slay him is almost an act of murder. To crucify him is—what?).[18] This kind of connection does not fit the subject in question, since it can never provide that particular adroitness of ingenuity which allows it to cause wonder.

Another kind of connection of things is intelligible, that is, "internal", since it does not depend upon any of the senses, but can only be understood by the intellect. This kind of connection is of two kinds: one simple, and without medium, which, to use terms drawn from logic, regards the second operation of the intellect. It consists in the simple predicating and conjunction of one thing with another by means of the verb. Let us call it a simple enunciation. Of this kind are the words of Aristotle: "regnum spontanea dominatio est" (kingly government is spontaneous domination),[19] Another kind joins things through a medium or through a cause, explicitly or implicitly. This is the third operation of the intellect according to the logicians, who normally call it a "syllogism". Among the rhetoricians, it is normally called "enthymeme". The simple, assertive connection cannot in any way contain any artifice, except through the application of words or idioms to new things, and this has already been considered above. Furthermore, I shall note that such a connection can never be simply enunciative, but will always and necessarily contain a tacit enthymematic force, since it relates two separate things through a third one.

Let us consider as an example of the enthymematic connection the one which Aristotle offers when he says: "Si deceptione quis aut vi dominetur, apparet hanc esse tyrannidem" (If someone rules with fraud and force, then it is evident that his rule is tyranny).[20] In this statement the parts are enthymatically joined together because of an implicit premise, that is, kingly government is domination over people who are content with it. As far as the intellect is concerned, this connection in which two things are conjoined to one another through an explicit or an implicit middle term, cannot provide any other artifice than that which, to use the terms of logic, is taught in syllogistic rules according to the proverb "de omni et de nullo" (by all and by none).

This kind of connection can, nevertheless, produce pleasure depending on the matter which it uses, owing to the great sagacity of the intellect such as is rarely seen in the invention of the middle term, and also owing to the quality of the things which it teaches, but not because it opens any ingenious perspective. Here the intellect does not really create, but only unveils and presents. Therefore, the operation of the intellect is not the most important object in the awareness of the audience or the reader, but the truth demonstrated alone is the object that matters. Indeed, truth has a very delightful face; nevertheless, it is a delight different from the kind which I am intending to pinpoint here. A proposition by Euclid delights you if your mind is able to grasp it, but such a delight is different from the one which you may experience when hearing an ingenious epigram by Martial. In brief, style has its role not only or principally in discovering beautiful things, but also in devising them; and the object of the plausible in our enquiry does not belong to the intellect, which only seeks truth and knowledge of things, but, rather, to ingenuity, which both in operating and as well in its enjoyment has as its object not so much truth, as beauty.

Therefore, the rarity of the invention in the enthymematic connection which matters here, should not so much be explained by the finding of a perfect junction of a middle term with the mediated terms,[21] as by the creation of a decorous, very rare and outstanding form of expression. When the joining middle term and the mediated terms are represented in their natural order, nothing rare can be created; and when artifice is completely absent, you cannot hope for anything but a good and clear syllogistic connection. And this will satisfy the intellect, but will not satisfy ingenuity at all. It is therefore necessary that either the middle terms or the mediated terms, or both, are well–devised, and, as the rhetorician would say, *figurati* [i.e. forming a rhetorical figure]. And since the art does not have any special, certain and easy rules such as may represent the above said parts with such rarity that from it a very gracious and befitting form of expression may arise, the whole business depends on the power of ingenuity, which cannot be wondrous unless by operating in an excellent way where there are no specific rules for operating well. When the figured connection succeeds in forming a very rare and befitting form of expression between the connected parts, so that the force of ingenuity shows itself as the main object of marvellousness in this act, we shall have the wondrous *acutezza*. This clearly seems to be the conclusion of the considerations undertaken so far.

Now, that in the kind of *acutezza* in question, force is given by an impressive artifice, which is expressed by terms connected to each other through an impressive and rare *acconcezza*[22] rather than by a great syllogistic force of connection, can be clearly seen in the following comparison: Ausonius said: "Sanus piger est febriente multo nequior: /potat duplum dapesque duplices devorat" (A lazy healthy man is much more needy than a sick one:/ he drinks twice as much and he eats twice as many meals).[23] When Nero sent Otho Silvius to the prefecture of Portugal in order to have a good time with his wife Poppaea without having a rival around, a witty person said: "Cur Otho mentito sit, quaeritis, exul honore? :/ Uxoris moechus coeperat esse suae" (You ask why Otho has been sent in exile under pretence of a false honour? He had begun to act as an adulterer to his wife).[24] When Claudius, general of the Roman army in the first of the Carthaginian Wars, was informed that the birds from which forecast should be made concerning the intended operation did not want to peck up food, but had dived into the sea as if commanded, he said: "Se non vogliono mangiar, bevano" (If they do not want to eat, then they must drink).[25] If you compare the *acutezza* of the second and third sayings with that of the first one, you will easily see that the second saying is more sparkling than the first: and this is despite the fact that the syllogistic connection seems more perfect in the first than in the second and the third sayings. Therefore such *acutezza* depends upon the use of the most figurative words, since, as everyone can see for himself, the second and the third greatly exceed the first in figurativeness, though they, on the other hand, are very inferior if compared to the enthymematical perfection. I mean figured with such style that a mutual *acconcezza*, grand and rare, may descend from it. Otherwise, it would not be relevant to our purpose. And although the *acconcezza*, which derives from its being impressive, will often be rare too, this is not necessary, for in this respect what is rare is not only perfect but also far from ordinary imagination.

From this it becomes possible to understand the nature of the particular skill of ingenuity, by which the *acutezza* is created. Because, just as Aristotle defined the skill of the intellect as a promptness to find successfully the middle term to make the demonstration,[26] so we shall be able to define the skill of ingenuity relative to our discussion as a successful invention of a middle term connecting figuratively different things in a saying with marvellous aptness. This readiness, this happy invention, you will necessarily understand by taking into consideration that which would be thought of by ordinary intellects and wits. Furthermore, one can come to understand the source of the wondrous, which consists in this distance from the common: because, as Aquinas said correctly, novelty and distance from the ordinary possess the power to cause wonder.[27] It also follows that the wondrous *acutezza* is much more based upon appearance than upon reality. This is so because the task of *acconcezza* is that of pleasing and making itself admired by listeners. But being gracious and wondrous does not necessarily need reality; on the contrary, the wondrous is all the more wondrous inasmuch as it is based upon appearance rather than on substance.

What I mean, though, is an impressive appearance, a condition which, at least through the figurative expression, will bring with it a solid reference to reality. If not, a feeble and obviously sophistic appearance cannot bring forth any rarity of *acconcezza*, and will therefore be somewhat affected, childish and vulgar, being in no case ingenious. An appearance which is unimpressive, cannot be wondrous, and when for some reason or other it reflects a particular work of ingenuity, we will not define it as a work of skill, but as a work of affectation.

These points are in accordance with the doctrines of the ancient philosophers, especially those of Aristotle and Cicero. They are in accordance with the doctrine of Aristotle, who expressedly stated that gracious statements are works of a mind, which is sagacious by nature or cultivated by study. He also said that the ability to see correspondences between different things is characteristic of a clever mind, and that devising the middle term to connect different things in a suitable way is nothing but finding such suitability in the expression.[28] Therefore, also for this reason our description of the skill of ingenuity comes to be in agreement with the Aristotelian discernment. These points of ours are similarly in agreement with the doctrine of Cicero, who, among the reasons for which he regards the use of *acutezze* as becoming the orator, he indicates the following one: "because everyone admires the acuteness, which is often concentrated in one single word."[29] And later on, when explaining why "ambiguities" are "extremely acute", and why "ambiguity delights extraordinarily by itself', he writes: "For it is typical of a witty man to know how to divert the force of word into a sense quite different from that in which the others expect him to take it; yet, this jest arouses more wonder than laughter."[30]

From these modes of speaking we learn three things. Firstly, that *acutezze* please inasmuch as they are admired. Secondly, that the main object of this delightful wonder is the particular power of the person who speaks. Thirdly, that this power and special ability is explained by considering the ability to bring together things which are far from the ordinary perception, for which it becomes worthy of admiration. This means that in an *acutezza* the principal object is the power of ingenuity, and, so to speak, its very same soul; this is also reflected by the words which we use to call it. For vivacity, wit, conceits and all similar nouns which are commonly used in relation to this sort of thing are all of such a nature that in one way or another they convey something vital. I do not know what this is, except the above–mentioned skill of ingenuity. And it is also in accordance with the main effect of similar wondrous *acutezze*, which are designed to please in a flattering manner. Because just as the corporeal eye does not come across any sight as exquisite as that of beautiful eyes, so it is equally acceptable that ingenuity, the eye of the mind, cannot meet any beam of beauty which is as exquisite to its taste as that which graciously burns in another ingenious mind. This is what concord between the interior and exterior part of man seems to require; the same applies to the reasons of the similar and the perfect, which it is the task of the metaphysical school to consider.

Notes

1 *Acutezza* may refer to a sentence (acute saying) or to a cognitive ability (acuteness).
2 See Quintilian, *Institutio oratoria* 1.6.32: "Pravis ingeniis ad foedissima usque ludibria labuntur." This note and some of the following ones are quoted from Ezio Raimondi's edition of M. Peregrini, *Delle acutezze*. See bibliography.
3 See Petronius, *Satyricon*, § 2: "Pace vestra dixerim, primi omnium eloquetiam perdidistis; levibus atque inanibus sonis ludibria quaedam excitando effecistis ut corpus orationis enervaretur et caderet."
4 "...non semper numero...concinnitate quadam, et constructione verborum." Peregrini paraphrases Cicero, *Orator* 49.164.
5 "...cum aut par pari aut contrarium contrario opponitur." Paraphrasing Cicero, *Orator* 49.164.
6 Rhetorical figure in which two words with similar sound, but different meaning, are joined.
7 See Quintilian, *Institutio oratoria* 9.3.70. In both examples there is a play upon words similar in sound but different in meaning: in the first example the verb "amare", to love, is similar in sound to the adjective "amarus", bitter. In the second example there is likewise a similarity in sounds between "avis", bird, and "avium", wilderness.
8 See Quintilian, *Institutio oratoria* 9.3.69.
9 In this example we find a repetition of sounds, stressing the paragone: the sounds of "mellificatis apes", honey–making of bees, is very similar to those of the words "nidificatis aves", the nest–making of birds. Quoted from *Vitae Vergilianae*, edited by E. Diehl, Bonn, Marcus u. Weber, 1912, p. 31.
10 See Cicero, *Ad familiares* 10.35.5.
11 See Sallust, *Bellum Catilinae* 54.2.
12 See Suetonius, *De vita caesarum* 34.2.
13 *Ibid.*, *De vita caesarum* I.80.3.
14 Macrobius, *Saturnalia* 2.2.4: "Sacrifice for the road": "propter viam".
15 See Suetonius, *De vita caesarum* 2.85.2.
16 See Ateneaeus, *Deipnosophistai* 6.47.245f.
17 See Florus, *Epitomae de Tito Livio bellorum omnium annorum DCC*, 1.24.17.
18 See Cicero, *In Verrem* 2.5.66.170.
19 See Aristotle, *Politics* 1313a.
20 *Ibid.*
21 With the expressions "middle term" and "mediated terms" Peregrini refers to the syllogism: "mediated terms" are the nouns or subjects presented in the two premisses of the syllogism; "middle term" is the predicate which unites these two nouns or subjects and makes a conclusion possible.
22 *Acconcezza* is an untranslatable word in this context. It means, roughly, apt and decorous dressing of the expression.
23 See Ausonius, *Epigrammata* 23.4.
24 See Suetonius, *Vitae caesarum*; *Otho* 7.3.2.
25 Valerius Maximus 1.4.3.
26 See Aristotle, *Posterior analytics* 89b.

27 Aquinas, *Summa theologia*, I, I, q. 105, art. 4 ad 4.
28 See Aristotle, *Rhetoric* 1410; 1412a.
29 See Cicero, *De oratore* 2.58.236: "Quia admirantur omnes acumen uno saepe in verbo positum."
30 See Cicero, *De oratore* 2.62.253–4: "Ambiguum per se probetur vel maxime. Ingeniosi enim esse videtur vim verbi in aliud atque caeteri accipiunt ducere posse; sed magis admirationem quam risum habet."

B. Extracts from

Emanuele Tesauro

THE ARISTOTELIAN TELESCOPE

On Argutezza and Its Parts in General

A divine product of the mind, better known for its expressions than for
its genesis, has in every century and among all men been admired to such
an extent that, when encountered through reading or listening, it is
received as a strange wonder with great joy and applause even by those
who do not know it. This product is *argutezza,*[1] the great mother of every
ingenious saying; the most shining light of oratory and poetic elocution;
the vital spirit of dead pages, the most pleasant dressing of civil
conversation, the highest effort of the intellect, the imprint of divinity in
the human soul. There is no river of eloquence so sweet as not to seem to
us dull and unattractive if it is without this sweetness of *argutezza*; no
flower can be found on Parnassus, however delicate, which has not been
transplanted from the gardens of *argutezza*; no solid force of a rhetorical
enthymeme[2] exists, which would not seem crushed and impotent without
this sharpness; no people so brutish and inhuman can exist, whose
dreadful faces do not brighten up with a friendly smile when these
flattering mermaids appear. Angels themselves, Nature and the
magnificent God, have expressed themselves through verbal or symbolic
argutezze when communicating to men their most recondite and
important secrets.

But, not only because of this divine Persuasion[3] does the speech
of ingenious men differ from that of plebeians, inasmuch as the speech of
Angels differs from that of men: through her wondrous power mute
things speak, senseless things come to life, dead ones rise again. Tombs,
sculptures and statues, having received voice, spirit and movement from
this enchantress of souls, ingeniously converse with ingenious men. In
brief, only that which is not enlivened by *argutezza* is really dead.

The truth is, desirous reader, that to the same extent as *argutezza* is shining and vivid, I found (as I told you) that among authors its origin is obscure, its essence unknown and its art is in a hopeless state. I have read many oratorical works, many epic, many lyrical, many dramatic ones, as well as many inscriptions, both ancient and modern, which are exquisitely adorned by flowers of this kind; but those very same authors who knew how to compose in a witty way, did not know what *argutezza* was, similar to blind Homer, who, as they say, knew what 'rosy', but not what 'a rose' was. Many ancient authors have started to take up the task of writing about *argutezze*, but in fact their entire discourse consists only in providing many ridiculous and facetious fruits by means of examples (such fruits being a small part of *argutezza*). But they undertake no discussion of the root, which is the highest genus, nor of the principal branches, which are the corresponding divisions of its species. Even Tully, who had no more difficulty in speaking wittily than in opening his mouth, after great discourses concludes that nature, not art, is the teacher of *argutezza*.[4] And although he puts before us a good bunch of acute and ingenious remarks, for all that he has not demonstrated, nor recognised, their place of origin. As if *argutezza* were a Nile, whose affluents are known, but whose source is not. In fact, although he mocked those who had attempted to investigate the track of witty jokes, he found nothing ridiculous in that art other than the folly of striving to reduce it to an art.[5]

On the other hand, divine Aristotle inspired me immensely and gave me great expectations for the investigation of the source of this art, because he minutely searched for all secrets of rhetoric and taught them to all those who listened to him attentively. So, we may call Aristotle's *Rhetoric* a very lucid telescope to examine all the perfections and imperfections of eloquence. When speaking about the whole of the art of rhetoric—which many said was not teachable except by Mother Nature—he said that this art could certainly be found by those who, having set themselves different compositions as their tasks (of which, whether by chance or skill, some are good and others bad), know by their judgements how to investigate, in a subtle manner, the reasons why some are excellent and some defective, why some make us sick and some call forth our applause.[6] It was, thus, with such expectations and with this author as my only guide, that I set out, while still young, to undertake an inquiry into such a noble and ingenious faculty, in order to add this supreme ornament to the *humanae litterae*, which in our century have been happily elevated to such glory by some noble minds of my country. I therefore composed an accurate volume in good Latin on the art of *argutezza*, which, together with my other rhetorical labours, still lies unpublished. And, lest my art of *argutezza* should appear debased to your eyes because of the insipidness of my own literary works, I made the same protestation as my author, who also taught how to recite, but never recited; who taught poetics, but never wrote any poems; who taught about *argutezze*, but never produced any, sharing this very glory with Isocrates, that he knew how to teach, but not how to practise, whereas Isocrates knew how to practise but not to how teach.[7]

Now, having begun—after being greatly urged to do so by many friends—to allow publication only of the small volume about *imprese*, a minor part of *argutezza*, it has subsequently been imposed upon me by the one who is master of my will,[8] to treat, entirely in Italian, for the sake of the courtiers, the two most pleasant arts, the symbolic and the lapidarian. These two comprise all the *argutezze* of words and figures: the symbolic *argutezze* are found in epigrams, epitaphs, eulogies, and in every kind of witty inscriptions; the lapidarian ones in *imprese*, emblems, back of medals, and in every sort of witty symbol.[9] So I found myself constrained to make use of my own labours in this enterprise, repeating many useful pieces of information about *argutezze*, in order to apply them to the making of symbols and inscriptions, the beautiful and witty family of such an illustrious mother...

Human 'Arguzie'

But now to come to human *arguzie*,[10] our last topic, about which we shall only speak briefly here, since comments on these have been made throughout the book. Since we are dealing with the efficient causes of *argutezze* at the moment, this is the proper place to reflect upon what sort of men are most disposed to produce them. When talking about metaphor, which (as we suggested above and as we shall demonstrate below) we may call the magnificent mother of all *argutezze*, our author explains to us that three things, whether separated or joined, fertilize the human mind with marvellous sayings: namely, ingenuity, fury and exercise.[11] Consequently, three kinds of persons are most disposed to the making of symbolic expressions; the ingenious, the furious and the trained.

Natural ingenuity is a marvellous force of the intellect, comprising two natural capacities: perspicacity and versatility. Perspicacity is the ability to penetrate into the most distant and minute circumstances of any subject, such as substance, matter, form, accident, attribute, causes, effects, purposes, sympathies, similar, superior, inferior, signs, definite nouns and synonyms, all of which lie entangled and hidden in any subject matter, as we shall say in its proper place.

Versatility is the ability to compare rapidly all these things, with one another or with the subject matter: it relates or separates them, it increases or decreases them, it deduces one from another, it hints to one by means of another, and with wondrous skill it replaces one with another, as do the jugglers in their calculations. And this is metaphor, the mother of poetry, of symbols and of *imprese*. And, as we shall see, he who is able to grasp and connect the most remote things, is the most ingenious maker of *arguzie*.

Therefore, no small difference is to be found between prudence and ingenuity, since ingenuity is more discerning, prudence is more mindful; ingenuity is more rapid, prudence is more steady; ingenuity reflects upon phenomena, prudence upon truth; and where the latter holds utility as its purpose, the former aspires to admiration and public applause. It is not, therefore, without reason that ingenious men were called divine; because, just as God creates *ex nihilo*, an ingenious person makes being out of non–being. He turns a lion into a man and an eagle into a city; he grafts a woman onto a fish and makes a mermaid into a symbol for an adulator. He combines the upper part of a goat with the tail of a serpent, and makes a chimera a hieroglyph for 'madness'. For which reason some of the ancient philosophers called ingeniousness a sparkle of the divine mind, and others a gift sent from God to his beloved. Although, to tell the truth, God's friends ought to ask with more fervent prayers for prudence rather than for ingenuity, since prudence has control over fortune, while ingenious persons are unlucky (unless a miracle occurs), and whereas the former conducts men to dignity and justness, the latter sends men to hospital. But since many prefer the glory of ingenuity to the many benefits of fortune, I shall say that the most ingenious men must have received a greater disposition to *argutezze* from nature. Indeed saying 'arguto' equals saying 'ingenious'...

Treatise on Metaphor

Finally, we have reached the summit of ingenious figures, step by step, in comparison with which all the other figures considered so far lose their merit, since metaphors are the most ingenious and acute, the most rare and wondrous, the most jolly and valuable product of human intellect. Truly an extremely ingenious product; if ingenuity consists in connecting together distant and separated ideas of the subject matter (as we said), then this is exactly the task undertaken by a metaphor, and by no other figure: drawing the mind, no less than the word, from one genus to another, it expresses one concept through another very different one, and thus finds similarity in dissimilar things. Therefore our author concludes that the making of metaphors is the labour of a sharp and most lively mind.[12] As a consequence, metaphor is the most acute figure of all, since the other figures are formed in an almost grammatical manner, and stop at the surface of a word, while a metaphor, in a thoughtful manner, penetrates into and examines the most abstruse notions in order to combine one with another; and while the other figures dress up concepts with words, metaphor dresses up words themselves with concepts.

Metaphor is therefore the most rare figure owing to the novelty produced by an ingenious combination. Without this novelty, ingenuity loses its glory and metaphor its force. For this reason our author warns us that metaphor alone is to be produced by us, and not borrowed from anyone else, as if it were a stolen baby.[13] And this novelty produces wonder,[14] when the listener in his mind—overwhelmed by the above–mentioned novelty—ponders over the acuteness of the ingenious image–maker and the unexpected image of the represented object.

For if a metaphor is so admirable, it is also, necessarily, genial and delightful, since wonder produces delight, as you experience from unexpected changes of scenes and performances which were never seen before. The reason is that, if (as our author teaches us),[15] the delight brought about by rhetorical figures stems from the desire of the human mind to learn new things without tiring oneself out, and to learn many things in a short time, then surely metaphor is the most delightful of all ingenious figures. By making our mind move from one genus to another as in a flight,[16] metaphor makes us see more than one object through one single word. For example, if you say: "Prata amoena sunt" (The meadows are pleasant), the only thing you do is to show me green meadows; but if you say: "'Prata rident" (The meadows are smiling), then (as I said) you will make me see the earth as an animated man, the meadow being the face, and the pleasantness being a cheerful smile. So in one small word all these notions of different genera emerge: earth, meadow, pleasantness, man, soul, smile, cheerfulness. And reciprocally, in a short glimpse I see on the human face the notions of meadows and all the relations which exist between these several notions, which I did not notice before. And this is the rapid and easy teaching by which delight is noticed, when to the mind of the listener a theatre full of wonders appears in but one word.

Nor is a metaphor less delightful to those who produce it than to those who listen to it. For a metaphor frequently assists, in a provident manner, to overcome the poverty of language, and, where the proper word is missing, it provides the necessary transferred word. It is as if you would like to say "vites gemmant" (the vines put forth buds), or "sol lucem spargit" (the sun strews light)[17] with plain words, You would not be able to do so. Therefore Cicero was right in pointing out that metaphors resemble those garments which, having been found out of necessity, also serve as pomp and ornament...[18]

The Marvellous

But now I want to reveal to you the most abstruse and secret product of human ingenuity, but also the most miraculous and fertile one, which has remained nameless in the schools of rhetoric, although it was well known by our author in his *Poetics*,[19] where it has its proper place. Generated by this figure, it generates many other figures, of the most beautiful kind, which fly about in prose and poetry alike. This is the figure which we may call, with a Greek term, *thauma*, that is, "the marvellous", which consists in a representation of two almost incompatible concepts, and therefore especially admirable, as in the saying about Xerxes, which was much praised by our author: "Per terras navigavit, per maria pedibus incessit" (He sailed on land, he walked on the sea); and this other one: "Aeneum vidi virum viro conglutinatum" (I saw a man of bronze united with another man),[20] and other infinite similar representations, in which the positive is joined with the negative or the positive with the positive or the negative with the negative.

Aristotle provides an example in the third book of his *Rhetoric* of the positive joined with the negative, where he calls the arch "a lyre without strings",[21] and in the *Poetics*, where he calls the bowl "a shield, not for war but for Bacchus".[22] This figure of speech is called by him a "metaphor consisting of two",[23] since it contains two incompatible and enigmatic terms which, as such, produce wonder. But since this miraculous man is want to point only at the vestiges of his doctrines in order that we ourselves may follow their track, as those of wild beasts are shown to hunting dogs, we must use our own ingenuity to extend what he says here about an enigmatic and wondrous metaphor to any proposition which may cause wonder by means of the coupling of two incompatible terms, of which one is positive and the other negative. So it is that, when speaking about the echo which repeats our voices from woods or cliffs, you may say: "Echo is a soulless soul, dumb and yet eloquent, that speaks without having a tongue; a man, and yet not a man, who produces sounds without a breath; an image without a shape, that paints sounds in the air without any colours. It is not your daughter and you have begotten her; you hear it and do not see it, it replies to you and does not hear you; it is a nothing speaking that does not know how to speak and yet speaks, or speaks without knowing what it is saying. It has not studied Latin or Greek, and yet speaks Latin and Greek." All propositions are wondrous, but nonetheless true.

As for the joining of the positive with the positive: "Echo is a nymph of the air, a speaking stone, an animated cliff, breath's daughter: she lives in the woods and speaks all languages. She is a wild sibyl who answers from caverns. She is a flatterer and a scorner in one person, who laughs if you laugh, cries if you cry, sings if you sing, blames you if you blame her, praises you if you praise her. She only lives as long as you speak: she breathes with your breath, reflects with your language, lives through your life. Only one lives but two speak. Only one speaks, answering himself. She is your double; and if you leave, she leaves; if you return, she returns: and if you die, she dies."

On the uniting of the negative with the negative: "She is neither man nor beast. She is neither capable of speaking nor of being silent. She neither knows how to lie nor how to speak truthfully. She is not speechless and yet without language. She is not locked up but cannot leave her shelter. She does not listen to you, neither do you see her: and yet, she answers you and you listen to her."

From these examples you can understand that there are as many differences as there are categories of these wondrous sayings, since they are all representations either of the physical matter, such as "man, not man"; or of metaphysical essence, such as "formless form", "she is your double"; or of quantity: "only one lives but two speak"; or of qualities: "a flatterer and scorner in one person"; or of relations: "likeness of the voice, daughter of the breath"; or of actions: "she cries if you cry, laughs if you laugh"; or of time: "she only lives as long as you speak"; or of place: "she is a wild sibyl who answers from caverns"; or of movement: "if you leave, she leaves"; or of instruments: "she speaks without language." And many other such figures are made of mixed categories, such as this one: "she lives in the woods and speaks all languages", which is a compound of time and action...

Concerning Metaphorical Arguments and True Concepts

Now, having reflected upon these witty sayings and having discussed this matter theoretically, I shall say that perfect wits and ingenious concepts are nothing but urbanely fallacious arguments. And principally you will agree with me that not every argument is witty, though ingenious. Because, if you quote that famous theorem of Euclid for me, that "in a triangle all three sides are equal because all the lines which are drawn directly from the centre to the circumference are equal", then I shall say that this is a truly ingenious piece of mathematical speculation, but not a witty one. And similarly, if I asked you for what reason the hail falls during the summer and not during the winter, should you reply to me that the second region[24] of air in winter is warm, and cold during the summer because of the antiperistasis,[25] and that therefore the vapour which is there freezes during the summer and not during the winter, this would by all means be a truly beautiful and learned meteorological answer; but you would not place it among those witty answers, nor would you call it an epigrammatic concept, even if you dressed it in a poetic metre, since the reason is in itself true and conclusive, even without any invention of the intellect. It is therefore necessary that a witty argument gains its force through ingenuity, that is, through some subtle invention, so that it truely may be called one of our concepts. It is for this reason that Macrobius, using the Greek term, called witty remarks *scommata*,[26] that is, jests; and in his *Ethics*[27] our author, when talking about urban man and ingenuity, quick to deliver witty remarks, called him *euscoptonta*,[28] that is, "a good jester",[29] and Seneca defined *argutezze* as "clever and subtle conclusions",[30] that is, paralogisms,[31] corresponding exactly to the final words of epigrams. And in order that you may realise that this is true, recall the examination of those ten *argutezze* which I have presented for you as examples. Each of them, unfolded in verses, would form a witty epigram, and you will find that they are all based upon one or another of the fallacious *topoi*, which our author called "*topoi* of apparent enthymemes".[32] The reason is that these enthymemes surprise the intellect, first appearing effective, but once examined attentively they dissolve into empty fallacies: just as the apples from the Black Sea appear beautiful and colourful; but if you taste them, they leave the teeth filled with ash and smoke...

Therefore I shall conclude by saying that the only praise for *argutezze* consists in knowing how to lie well. Such a glory was fully attributed by our author to the good Homer, to which he added that the lies of poets are but paralogisms.[33] And the Muses boasted of this same glory in Hesiod, when they said: "we know how to tell very plausible lies..."[34]

But I seem to hear you say: "So, all the fallacious sophisms of dialecticians and the condemned quibbles of Protagoras and Zeno[35] should be regarded as witty remarks and ingenious concepts, belonging to the category of epigrams." A substantial and vast difficulty, but which our oracle solved in just two words: "witty enthymeme."[36] Truly, in order to understand them well, it would be useful to explain all the arcane mysteries in the whole of the art of rhetoric, mysteries which are still today entangled in many most intricate questions: mainly, what difference exists between dialectic and rhetoric, the two sisters who (as our author remarks wittily),[37] were born in one single childbirth and who resemble each other so much that many teachers take one for the other. But to give you, in passing, a brief example taken from our oracle himself, I shall tell you that the urbane jest is different from the dialectical ones in relation to subject matter, aim, as well as accidental and essential forms.

I claim that dialectic and rhetoric differ regarding subject matter. Because (as I shall explain more fully elsewhere) rhetoric comprises things of civic interest inasmuch as they depend upon moral persuasion, thus falling under the three above–mentioned genera of praising or blaming, advising or warning, and accusing or defending, both in private business and civil conversations, as well as in public speeches. Dialectic, on the other hand, comprises matters debatable in the scholastic institutions among searchers of truth. Therefore, the sentence "Verres is an individual composed of body and rational soul", belongs to dialectic; but the sentence "Verres is one of Sicily's public thieves", falls into rhetoric. So, rhetorical jest is based on topics calling for popular acceptance, whereas a dialectical jest is based on topics that can be debated in the scholastic institutions. So, if you said to me: "Being is a syllable; but being is a genus: therefore a syllable is a genus",[38] this would be a dialectic paralogism pertaining to a scholastic subject matter, which does not offend anyone. But if you said: "Verres", i.e. the pig,[39] "is a wild beast; but Verres rules Sicily: therefore a wild beast rules over Sicily", this would be a paralogism similar to the dialectical one, as far as the topical place is concerned, that is, in equivocation, as well in the syllogistic figure; but it would nevertheless be a rhetorical paralogism as far as its subject matter is concerned, because it vituperates the praetor of Sicily.

Consequently, rhetoric and dialectic are different regarding their respective aims. Because, just as rhetoric is concerned with persuasion of people and dialectic with scholastic teaching, so an urbane witticism aims at pleasing the soul of the listener by means of pleasantness and without hindrance of truth; but the dialectical witticism aims at corrupting the good reasoning of disputants by means of falseness, in the manner of jugglers. It is for this reason that our author recommends that the rhetorician should know how to produce sophisms in his persuasive intent and how to use them: because, even when he argues in favour of something honourable, he is allowed to use any argument. On the contrary, the dialectician knows well how to produce sophisms, but he is not allowed to use them, since it would be a disgrace for him to search for truth and teach falseness. Of this kind was the paralogism which Zeno called his "Achilles": dialectical deception[40] with which he pretended to convince his pupils that nothing whatsoever could move, neither in heaven nor on earth, although the eyes warrant that things move: "every continuum is composed of individuals; but apart from the individual nothing moves: therefore, apart from the continuum, nothing moves."[41] Such were also the jests of Protagoras, who is criticised by Aristotle[42] as a shameless manipulator of talents and an oppressor of truth by means of falseness. And also those of Aeschines, whom Demosthenes compares to the ruthless mermaids,[43] since with his paralogism he did not intend to encourage to useful things, but to make them precipitate dangerous ones.

Also regarding the material form the urbane enthymeme is different from the dialectical sophism, since the aim of the rhetorician is to persuade in any manner which is most pleasing to the listener, even using brief fictitious stories and inventions, the rhetorician will sometimes flavour the sentences of his enthymemes with beautiful phrases, whereas some other time he will hand them to us without any dialectical order; now he will cut out those phrases which the listener, knowing them already, would not hear without getting bored, and now he will entangle those which, being unfolded and clear, would make the fallacy clear. On the contrary, among disputants, who carefully refine their knowledge of truth, the propositions in the syllogism must be clear and explicit, in order that the intellect, when accepting the antecedent, is forced to accept what follows from it. Hence, in Cicero's jest against the edict of Verres you will see an enthymeme completely wrapped up and swiftly striking in a few words: "Mirandum non est ius Verrinum tam esse nequam" (Each Piggish edict should not be admired since it is vile).[44] If he had unfolded the enthymeme, it would have had this form as a dialectical syllogism:

> Omne ius verrium est nequam
> Sed edictum Verris est ius Verrinum
> Igitur edictum Verris est nequam,
>
> (Every piggish mud is vile
> But the edict of Verres is a piggish mud
> Therefore the edict of Verres is vile),

in which the equivocation of the middle term, "ius verrinum" (piggish mud), would have appeared too clearly; but in the enthymeme, wrapped up and only brought in if as in passing, it is overlooked by the listener and will surprise him, because he enjoys this dexterity of the intellect and laughs at it as if it were a good hand's trick.

The last and most important difference concerns the essential form of using witticisms, for even though every jest is a fallacy, any fallacy is not an urbane jest, but only that fallacy which, without evil malice, imitates truth in a joking manner, without oppressing it; it imitates falsehood in such a manner as to make truth visible behind it, as behind a veil, so that you will quickly understand that which is unspoken from that which is said. The real essence of metaphor consists in this rapid teaching (as we have demonstrated).[45] For this reason, just as in simple metaphors, when I say to you "prata rident" (the meadows smile), I do not intend to make you believe that the meadows laugh as men do, but that they are delightful—so the metaphorical enthymeme infers one thing in order that you may understand another. The rhetorical witticism does not want you to make you to believe that the edict of Verres really is some animal's disgusting mud; but under that metaphor of equivocation it wants you to understand the iniquity of that edict. And this is the witty jest which you asked me about. On the other hand, the dialectical jest is intended to make you take its propositions as they sound. And just as the rhetorical witty jest teaches you truth under cover of falsity, the dialectical jest impudently teaches you falsity under cover of truth. In brief, the difference between them is that between a true viper, which all of a sudden bites and poisons you, and a painted one, which looks as if it wants to bite you, and yet pleases you. For witty remarks are true products of poetry, whose essence is imitation. Summing up the four aspects which I have discussed with you, I shall conclude by saying that the urbane enthymeme is an ingenious jest which is related to civic subject matters, and is persuasive in a joking manner, which does not have the complete form of a syllogism, and is based on a metaphor. And this is the most perfect *argutezza*, about which we are speaking here.

Notes

1   *Argutezza* is an untranslatable word, meaning wit or witty saying.
2   A syllogism in an abbreviated form.
3   Called Pito in Italian. This name is derived from Greek, Πειτω. Among the Latins corresponding to Suada. This note, and some of the following ones, are quoted from Ezio Raimondi's edition of Tesauro's *Il cannocchiale aristotelico*. See bibliography.
4   Cicero, *De oratore* 2.54.216.
5   *Ibid.*, 2.54.216–218.
6   Aristotle, *Rhetoric* 1354a
7   Cicero, *Brutus* 8.32–34.
8   The prince Maurice of Savoy.
9   In "Impresa", p. 149, John A. Goodall defines *impresa* as a "personal or familial badge or device comprising a design accompanied by an apt word or brief motto suggesting in veiled terms its significance". *Imprese* are thus to be distinguished from emblems, which, according to Sinclair Hood in "Emblem book", p. 173, "consists of three parts: a short, often Classical, motto (*lemma, inscriptio*), a pictorial representation or icon (*pictura*) and the explanation of the link between them in an epigram (*subscriptio*)".
10 *Arguzia* is derived from *argutezza*, and it means witticism or sharpness.
11 See Aristotle, *Rhetoric* 1410b.
12 *Ibid.*, *Poetics* 1459a.
13 *Ibid.*, *Rhetoric* 1405a.
14 *Ibid.*, 1404b.
15 *Ibid.*, 1410b.
16 *Ibid.*, *Poetics* 1457b; *ibid.*, *Rhetoric* 1410b.
17 See Quintilian, *Institutio oratoria* 8.6.4–7.
18 Cicero, *De oratore* 3.38.155.
19 Tesauro may refer to Aristotle, *Poetics* 1459a.
20 See Aristotle, *Poetics* 1458a. Also quoted in *ibid.*, *Rhetoric* 1405b. The example refers to a cupping–bowl.
21 Aristotle, *Rhetoric* 1412b.
22 *Ibid.*, *Poetics* 1457b.
23 "Translatio ex duobus constans."
24 "Seconda region": see Seneca, *Naturales quaestiones* 4.3.1f.
25 "Antiperistasis": opposition of pressures.
26 "Scommata": jests. See Macrobius, *Saturnalia* 7.3.2.
27 Aristotle, *Nichomachean Ethics* 1128a.
28 "Euscoptonta": keen–sighted.
29 "Bonum cavillatorem."
30 "Conclusiunculae vafrae et callidae."
31 A piece of false reasoning.
32 "Apperentium enthumematum loci." See Aristotle, *Rhetoric* 1400b.
33 Aristotle, *Poetics* 1460a.
34 "Scimus mendacia dicere multum verisimilia." See Hesiod, *Theogony* 27.
35 They were masters in logic subtlety and in analysis of paradoxes.
36 "Enthymema urbanum." See Aristotle, *Rhetoric* 1410b.

37   *Ibid.*, 1354a.

38   "Ens syllaba est; sed ens est genus: ergo syllaba est genus."

39   A pun in Latin: from the name of the praetor Verres is derived an adjective,
     "Verrinus", meaning Verrine or belonging to Verres; this is similar to the adjective
     "verrinus", meaning piggish.

40   Fragment 25–26 in Zeno, see H. Diels, *Die Fragmente der Vorsokratier*, I, Berlin,
     1934, p. 253. Also in Aristotle, *Physics* 6.9.

41   "Omne continuum componitur ex individuis; sed super individuo nihil movetur:
     igitur super continuo nihil movetur."

42   Aristotle, *Rhetoric* 1402a.

43   See Aeschines, *Against Ctesiphon* 228.

44   This enthymeme and the following unfolded syllogism presupposes that the reader
     knows the Latin word "Verrinus": from the name of the praetor Verres is derived
     an adjective, "Verrinus", meaning Verrine or belonging to Verres; this adjective is
     similar to the adjective "verrinus", meaning piggish. Also, that "ius" can mean
     both "edict" and "mud".

45   See Aristotle, *Rhetoric* 1410b.

Literature Cited

PRIMARY SOURCES

If nothing else is indicated, all references to Vico are to the edition by G. Gentile and F. Nicolini, mentioned below. Similarly, if nothing else is stated, references to Tesauro are to the edition by E. Raimondi, likewise indicated below.

Arnauld, Antoine & Nicole, Pierre. *La logique ou l'art de penser* [1662]. Ed. C. Jourdain. Paris: Gallimard, 1992.

Descartes, René. *Discours de la méthode* [1637]. Ed. É. Gilson. Paris: J. Vrin, 1930.

Leibniz, Gottfried W. "Meditationes de cognitione, veritate et ideis" [1684]. In *Philosophische Schriften*, 2 vols. Ed. H. H. Holz. Darmstadt: Wissenschaftliche Buchgesellschaft, 1989, vol. 1.

Pallavicino, Sforza. *Trattato dello stile e del dialogo* [1662]. In *Trattatisti e narratori del seicento*. Ed. E. Raimondi. Milan and Bologna: Riccardo Ricciardi, 1960, pp. 197–217.

Peregrini, Matteo. *Delle acutezze, che altrimenti spiriti, vivezze e concetti volgarmente si appellano* [1639]. In *Trattatisti e narratori del seicento*. Ed. E. Raimondi. Milan and Bologna: Riccardo Ricciardi, 1960, pp. 113–168.

——. *I fonti dell'ingegno ridotti ad arte* [1650]. In *Trattatisti e narratori del seicento*. Ed. E. Raimondi. Milan and Bologna: Riccardo Ricciardi, 1960, pp. 169–190.

Tesauro, Emanuele. *Il cannocchiale aristotelico* [1654]. In *Trattatisti e narratori del seicento*. Ed. E. Raimondi. Milan and Bologna: Riccardo Ricciardi, 1960, pp. 19–106.

——. *Il cannocchiale aristotelico, o' sia, idea dell'arguta et ingegnosa elocutione, che serve à tutta l'arte oratoria, lapidaria, et simbolica, esaminata co' principii del divino Aristotele.* Halle, 1664.

Vico, G. B. *Opere*. 8 vols. Ed. G. Gentile and F. Nicolini. Bari: Laterza, 1914–1941.

——. *Opere*. 2 vols. Ed. Andrea Battistini. Milan: Mondadori, 1990.

——. *Oratio I*. Ed. Gian G. Visconti. In *Bollettino del centro di studi vichiani*, 5, 1975, pp. 4–39.

——. *Institutiones oratoriae*. Ed. G. Crifò. Naples: Istituto Suor Orsola Benincasa, 1989.

——. *The Art of Rhetoric ('Institutiones oratoriae', 1711-1741)*. Trans. and ed. Giorgio A. Pinton and Arthur W. Shippe. In *Value Inquiry Book Series*, nr. 37. Amsterdam and Atlanta: Rodopi, 1996.

SECONDARY LITERATURE

Battistini, Andrea & Raimondi, Ezio. *Le figure della retorica. Una storia letteraria italiana*. Turin: Einaudi, 1984.

Battistini, Andrea. "Acutezza." In *Historisches Wörterbuch der Rhetorik*. Offprint from vol. 1: A–Bib. Ed. G. Ueding. Tübingen: Max Niemeyer, 1992.

Brisca, L. Menapace. "L'arguta et ingegnosa elocuzione. Appunti per una lettura del 'Cannocchiale aristotelico' di E. Tesauro." In *Aevum*, nr. 28, 1954, pp. 45–60.

Cazzullo, Anna. *La verità della parola. Ricerca sui fondamenti filosofici della metafora in Aristotele e nei contemporanei*. Milan: Jaca Book, 1987.

Cesare, Donatella Di. "La filosofia dell'ingegno e dell'acutezza di Matteo Pellegrini e il suo legame con la retorica di Giambattista Vico." In *Prospettive di storia della linguistica*. Ed. Lia Fomigari and Franco Lo Piparo. Rome: Riuniti, 1988, pp. 157–173.

——. "Sul concetto di metafora in Giambattista Vico." In *Prospettive di storia della linguistica*. Ed. Lia Fomigari and Franco Lo Piparo. Rome: Riuniti, 1988, pp. 213–223.

Conte, Giuseppe. *La metafora barocca. Saggio sulle poetiche del seicento*. Milan: Mursia, 1972.

Corsano, Antonio. "Vico and Mathematics." In *Vico. An International Symposium*. Ed. G. Tagliacozzo and H. V. White. Baltimore: Johns Hopkins University Press, 1969, pp. 425–437.

——. *G. B. Vico*. Bari: Laterza, 1956.

Croce, Benedetto. *La filosofia di Giambattista Vico*. Bari: Laterza, 1911.

——. *Estetica come scienza dell'espressione e linguistica generale*. Bari: Laterza, 1909.

Croce, Franco. "Le poetiche del barocco in Italia." In *Momemti e problemi di storia dell'estetica*. Milan: Marzorati, 1959, pp. 547–575.

Curtius, E. Robert. *Europäische Literatur und lateinische Mittelalter*. Bern: Francke, 1948.

Garin, Eugenio. *L'umanesimo italiano. Filosofia e vita civile nel rinascimento*. Bari: Laterza, 1993.

——. *Storia della filosofia italiana*. Turin: Einaudi, 1966.

Gentile, Giovanni. *Studi vichiani* [1927]. Ed. V. A. Bellezza. In Giovanni Gentile, *Opere*, vol. XVI. Florence: Sansoni, 1968.

Gilbert, Neal W. *Renaissance Concepts of Method*. New York: Columbia University Press, 1960.

Giuliani, Alessandro. "Vico's Rhetorical Philosophy and the New Rhetoric." In *Giambattista Vico's Science of Humanity*. Ed. G. Tagliacozzo and D. P. Verene. Baltimore and London: Johns Hopkins University Press, 1976, pp. 31–46.

Goodall, John A. "Impresa." In *The Dictionary of Art*. 34 vols. Ed. Jane Turner. Ohio: Grove, 1996, vol. 15, pp. 149-151.

Gregory, Tullio. *Scetticismo ed empirismo. Studio su Gassendi*. Bari: Laterza, 1961.

Hood, Sinclair. "Emblem books." In *The Dictionary of Art*. 34 vols. Ed. Jane Turner. Ohio: Grove, 1996, vol. 10, pp. 173-177.

Koch, Carl Henrik. *Den europæiske filosofis historie*. Copenhagen: Arnold Busck, 1983.

Kristeller, P. Oskar. "The Modern System of Arts." In *Renaissance Thought II*. New York: Harper Torchbooks, 1965, ch. 9.

Kraye, Jill. "Philologists and Philosophers." In *The Cambridge Companion to Renaissance Humanism*. Ed. Jill Kraye. Cambridge: Cambridge University Press, 1996, pp. 142–160.

Lange, Klaus–Peter. *Theoretiker des literarischen Manierismus. Tesauros und Pellegrinis Lehre von der 'acutezza' oder von der Macht der Sprache*. Munich: Wilhelm Fink, 1968.

Lausberg, Heinrich. *Handbuch der literarischen Rhetorik*. Munich: Max Hueber, 1960.

Löwith, Karl. "Vicos Grundsatz: *verum et factum convertuntur*. Seine theologishe Prämisse und deren säkulare Konsequenzen." In

Sitzungsberichte der Heidelberger Akademie der Wissenschaften.
Heidelberg: Carl Winter Universitätsverlag, 1968, pp. 3–36.

Mooney, Michael. *Vico in the Tradition of Rhetoric.* New Jersey: Princeton, 1985.

——. "The Primacy of Language." In *Vico and Contemporary Thought.* London and Basingstoke: Macmillan, 1980, pp. 191–210.

Morpurgo–Tagliabue, Guido. "Aristotelismo e barocco." In *Retorica e barocco. Atti del III congresso internazionale di studi umanistici. Venezia 15.–18. giugno 1954.* Ed. E. Castelli. Rome: 1955, pp. 119–195.

——. *Anatomia del barocco.* Palermo: Aesthetica, 1987.

Nicolini, Fausto. *Commento storico alla seconda 'Scienza nuova'.* Rome: Storia e letterature, 1949.

Ong, Walter J. *Ramus. Method, and the Decay of Dialogue. From the Art of Discourse to the Art of Reason* [1958]. Cambridge, Massachusetts, Harvard University Press, 1983.

Panofsky, Erwin. *Idea. Eine Beitrag zur Begriffsgeschichte der älteren Kunsttheorie* [1924]. Berlin: Wissenschaftsverlag Volker Spiess, 1993.

Pareyson, Luigi. "La dottrina vichiana dell'ingegno." In *L'estetica e i suoi problemi.* Milan: Marzorati, 1961, pp. 351–377.

Pöggeler, Otto. "Vico e l'idea topica." In *Studi filosofici*, vol. 5 and 6, 1982–1983, pp. 65–81.

Prosatori latini del quattrocento. Ed. E. Garin. Milan and Naples: Riccardo Ricciardi, 1952.

Raimondi, Ezio. "Ingegno e metafora nella poetica del Tesauro." In E. Raimondi. *Lettura barocca. Studi sul seicento italiano.* Florence: Olschki, 1961.

Rummel, Erika. *The Humanist–Scholastic Debate in the Renaissance and Reformation.* Cambridge, Massachusetts and London: Harvard University Press, 1995.

Sorrentino, Andrea. *La retorica e la poetica di Vico. Ossia la prima concezione estetica del linguaggio.* Turin: Fratelli Bocca, 1927.

Struever, Nancy S. "Vico, Valla, and the Logic of Humanist Inquiry." In *Giambattista Vico's Science of Humanity.* Ed. G. Tagliacozzo and D.

P. Verene. Baltimore and London: Johns Hopkins University Press, 1976, pp. 173–185.

Toffanin, Giuseppe. *L'Arcadia.* Bologna: Zanichelli, 1958.

Vasoli, Cesare. *La dialettica e la retorica dell'umanesimo. 'Invenzione' e 'metodo' nella cultura del XV e XVI secolo.* Milan: Feltrinelli, 1968.

——. "Topica, retorica e argomentazione nella 'prima filosofia' del Vico." In *Revue internationale de philosophie*, vol. 33, 1979, nr. 127–130, pp. 188–201.

——. "Le imprese del Tesauro." In *Retorica e barocco. Atti del III congresso internazionale di studi umanistici. Venezia 15–18. giugno 1954.* Ed. E. Castelli. Rome: 1955, pp. 243–249.

Verene, Donald Phillip. *Vico's Science of Imagination.* Ithaca and London: Cornell University Press, 1981.

Index

The index covers the text as well as the appendix, though not the notes. Authors of secondary literature are mentioned in the index if I undertake a discussion with him or her. References to Vico are not indicated with a separate entry, since these references are pervasive; instead they are located according to their topic.

Emory Vico Studies

Donald Phillip Verene, General Editor

Emory Vico Studies is specifically associated with the Institute for Vico Studies at Emory University, Atlanta. The series welcomes submission of any book-length manuscripts on Vico or on literary or philosophical topics related to Vico and Vichian thought.

For further information about the Emory Vico Studies series and for the submission of manuscripts, contact:

Donald Phillip Verene
Emory University
Department of Philosophy
Institute for Vico Studies
Atlanta, GA 30322